The Prehistoric Rock Art of Kilmartin

KIL MAR TIN HOUSE

The Prehistoric Rock Art of Kilmartin
Stan Beckensall

This book is dedicated to those who have worked hard in the past to reveal the rich rock art heritage of Kilmartin - especially Marion Campbell of Kilberry and Ronald Morris - and to those who have been my companions in much of the search in the present: Paul and Barbara Brown. There are many others who have contributed to this work in their capacity as paid archaeologists, but there are also those who do it voluntarily, including Kaledon Naddair and his team.

Published by Kilmartin House Trust
Kilmartin, Argyll, PA31 8RQ, Scotland
Telephone: 01546 510278
http://www.kht.org.uk
ISBN 0-9533674-2-8

© 2005 Stan Beckensall. All rights reserved.
No part of this publication may be reproduced in any form or by any means – graphic, electronic or mechanical, including photocopying, recording, taping or information storage and retrieval systems – without the prior permission in writing of the publishers.
Registered Scottish Charity SC 022744

Contents

	Preface	4
1.	Introduction	7
2.	The lie of the land	11
3.	An overview of British Prehistoric Rock Art	15
4.	Setting the scene: Achnabreck	24
5.	From Lochgilphead to Dunamuck	34
6.	The Upper Add Glen	50
7.	The Fringes and Central Area of the Kilmartin Glen	57
8.	The West	90
9.	Loch Awe to Upper Largie	104
10.	Kilbride	113
11.	The East Coast	115
12.	The significance of the distribution of Rock Art in the region and its wider context	118
13.	The future of Rock Art studies	137
14.	Bibliography	141

Acknowledgements

Preface

Christopher Chippindale

They were born and they lived and they had their beings; they experienced joy and sadness, frights and hunger and pain; and they died – just as we have done and just as we do and just as we will do, except we know so much less or nearly nothing of hunger and pain. These are the prehistoric people of Scotland, the people whose names by definition we do not know, for prehistory is the time before history, the time before any historical records exist which can tell us the name of those people and the name of their country, the country that later was given the name of Caledonia for the area of Roman Britain north of the Antonine Wall.

The people of later prehistoric Scotland were – on the surface – people like us in other ways. They grew barley and – we researchers hope to deduce from ambiguous evidence – they knew how to brew with it. They had cattle and sheep and pigs. Even in the Neolithic, the first period of Scotland's farmers from around or before 3000 BC, they had rectangular houses.

Archaeology is the study of the past from the material evidence, so the archaeological study is one of physical evidence, from the bones and the stones and the pots. But what was it like to be Neolithic in Scotland? Here, the material evidence clearly shows how these were people also not like us. There are the houses, but very few of them even across the whole of the British Isles. Have the other houses perished? Were there never many? Did other things and other places mean more to Neolithic people, things and places which were of central value then but whose values mean nothing to ourselves today?

Kilmartin is rich in these other things and places. Chief amongst them are the great standing stones, blocks which were erected in the landscape singly, or in groups, or making lines and rings – stones which are the singular evidence of the Neolithic imagination, of the things that mattered to Neolithic existence.

Although transformed by centuries of human interference, the Kilmartin landscape also holds enduring evidence of how ancient Scots – or pre-Scots – marked its landscape. This is rock-art, the images which were cut into natural rock surfaces or painted on to natural rock surfaces nearly everywhere in the world where there have been people to mark and welcoming rock surfaces to be marked of a kind where the marks endure. In wet Britain, we have no ancient rock-paintings, for paint does not like open and wet places, but we do have a special tradition of marking in the rocks by pecking designs into them. Where some other European regions – famously the Pleistocene painted caves of France and Spain – are blessed with striking images of animals, nearly everything in the British rock-art tradition is more enigmatic, more reticent. The characteristic forms of our 'cup-and-ring' rock-art are the cups pecked out of the rock surface of a size and shape fitting or not to hold a golf ball, and the 'rings', circular forms which do or do not touch or enclose a cup and which do or do not multiply in concentric rings, and which are or are not further elaborated or connected by lines or other shapes. This art is distinctive in form, with even the several 'or nots' admitted, but hard to date reliably. And it offers no easy clues as to what it means or stands for. Often it is called 'abstract', but we do not even know that: the cups and rings may be geometric shapes made for their geometric shape alone – but they may equally be realistic images of things we do not grasp the shape of, or shapes which were full of specific meanings.

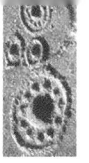

Whatever they are, the British rock-art markings have three characteristics which are true of rock-art nearly everywhere: they are very often fixed in place, marked on the living rock or into great boulders, rather than decorating small and portable artefacts; they are enduring in time, uncertainly dated but certain to be over 3000 years old; we can be pretty sure they were full of social meaning then; and they are full of social meaning in our own time. Stonehenge – another ancient place whose true prehistoric name we do not know, so we rename it in our own English tongue – each summer solstice receives 30,000 visitors who stay up all night to watch the sun rise, or not, over its ancient stones, in the mistaken belief this is the true prehistoric point of its ancient symmetry. The mistake is less important than the number, the number of people who find ancient meaning today in a usually mist- or cloud-obscured sunrise over the old stones.

Fortunately, the great Neolithic sites around Kilmartin are less known, less overwhelmed, and at the rock-art sites you will usually be lucky enough to be on or nearly on your own. Being on your own, pretty well, at these ancient places is something most of us prefer, as we sense – rightly or wrongly (I would guess wrongly) – that way helps us more to grasp the feel and force of the place. Still, it would be good to have a guide, a guide who will first find the place for us if we cannot find it: the first aspect to the reticence of British rock-art sites is the skill with which they hide themselves from the visitor!

I was lucky enough to grow up for some of my teen years, not in Scotland, but in that northern part of England whose rounded high hills resemble Scotland - rather than in that English soft south around London which northerners are rightly suspicious of. I knew nothing of rock-art then, and the Westmoreland fells of the high country I came to know are too rounded and of the wrong kind of rock, so they have no rock-art. What I did have there was good school-teachers, teachers with that kind of infective enthusiasm which inspired an otherwise rather confused teenager. If I close my eyes now, I can after thirty-seven forgetful years still see the face and the shape of his glasses and the way they framed his eyes, and I can hear the voice and remember the name of Mr Alban, the David Alban who taught me English.

So my ideal guide to the rock-art of Kilmartin would be a northern school-teacher, and by some human process which is clearly more significant than simple chance, that ideal guide exists. He is Stan Beckensall, the Northumberland school-teacher whose patient work has quietly revolutionized the study of British rock-art. He has found scores of new sites – the total number of rock-art sites known in his Northumberland is rising so far it threatens to reach a thousand over the next few years. He has recorded both old and new sites with photographs and rubbings, so our record of just what the motifs are has been transformed. And he has written engaging guidebooks, with good field instructions (so you find the sites), and with good illustrations of the figures (so you know what to look out for), and with good guidance about their archaeological context, and with sensible ideas about their possible meaning: another mark of the good school-teacher is their skill in holding back the teenagers when their enthused imagination starts to take them too far. A few of us have been lucky enough to go to the rock-art sites with Stan in person. More of us have been guided by his series of books, on the rock-art of Northumbria, of Cumbria, and of Durham and neighbouring Yorkshire dales. And now – bless him! – he has written this guide to the rock-art of Kilmartin.

Rock-art is enduring in time, so even ancient panels survive many generations after their makers passed on. If Kilmartin rock-art is of the order of 3000 years old, then we are perhaps 150 generations away from the people who made it, a number both startlingly large and startlingly small. No wonder we are so transformed from those first farmers whose plants and animals and houses appear on the surface to be like ours! But each of us resembles our parents more or less closely, or if not then we have usually reacted in a usually predictable way in how we do not resemble them, so how can just 150 of those close successions be enough so to make a complete transformation? Shouldn't we know about rock-art that way? Well we don't. A Beckensall is needed.

Like those pioneers in the Kilmartin landscape, who set up the stones, and who marked its rocks with their hollows and rings, Stan will not endure for ever. But, thanks to the thoroughness of his recording methods, his rubbings and photographs and careful written descriptions should last for generations into the future, even when the bulldozers and the acid rain and the grass and the roots have further transformed and rubbed away those marks in the land which Neolithic people shaped and left for us. Now and even when he has gone, as they did and as he will and as I will and we all will, with his book we can explore the Kilmartin rock-art with an expert and an enduring guide.

Cambridge University Museum of Archaeology & Anthropology
before the midsummer solstice, June 2004

1. Introduction

The area of Argyll centred on Kilmartin is one of the most interesting and important regions in Britain for its visible prehistoric remains. It is also one of the best for displaying them to the public, with signs denoting where monuments are and high quality display panels. Served by Kilmartin House Trust, the area has a museum which records and displays what is visible to visitors, and acts as a centre for further research.

This book has limited the study of prehistoric rock art to an area covered by the OS Explorer Series 358 map, Lochgilphead and Knapdale North. Visitors and researchers who wish to locate all recorded sites – small, overgrown and the less accessible – will find them here.

I have been visiting sites here for many years; making wax rubbings in preparation for accurate drawings, and taking digital, slide and print photographs. References have been chased up and 'lost' sites found. Some new sites have been recorded, while others have not been re-located. The purpose of this book is to make all that information available for a landscape that is varied and exciting; and to relate rock motifs to topography and to other prehistoric sites, for the position of markings follows some sort of logic. Viewpoints, loch-sides and special places such as stream sources are discussed, as are monumental contexts such as standing stones and burial cairns. Other decorated stones have been moved from their original places, and are here recorded as 'portables'.

1. Kilmartin Glen and Loch Awe

Above all, detailed illustrations are included so that readers will be able to see precisely what is on the rocks. Very often, especially when there is little oblique sunlight, one visit to a rock may not bring out the pattern on it. A careful, thorough rubbing (which comes with years of practice) can reveal more than the eye can normally see. Particularly important are any signs of the sequence in which markings were made, and which have suffered most from erosion. This information, checked by reference to photographs often taken when a rock surface is wet, is transferred to graph paper with the help of a squared 'grid', and then drawn.

Archaeologists do not work in isolation – they have so many sources to draw on, often the accumulation of many years' work by other people. In particular, in this area the Royal Commission on the Ancient and Historical Monuments of Scotland (1988) made a very important synthesis of all the information then available and ensured that photographs and drawings were of the highest quality. All of us have gleaned information from many sources, and owe much to Ronald Morris and to Marion Campbell of Kilberry for their coherent recording of what was known at the time.

Since the work of early pioneers, there has been considerable interest in rock art, and during the past 20 years it has ceased to be a Cinderella subject on the fringes of archaeology, and has become a major component of the archaeological record. Our approach to it has changed too. It is now studied in great detail to explain why it appears in particular locations. Although absolute dating is still not possible, it is now recognised as having had a use of over one thousand years, from the late Neolithic through the Early Bronze Age. It is one of the earliest forms of communication – visual, rather than oral – between prehistoric peoples and us. Simple in its symbolism, it has nevertheless become a basis for considerable differences in design by manipulating symbols. When markings take full advantage of the symbols available, the slope and surface of the rock, and of its place in the landscape or on a monument, it has an aesthetic appeal.

The Kilmartin area occupies an important place in British rock art; to detach it from other regions would be a mistake, for it is part of a wider phenomenon. We have long been aware of

2. Kilmartin Glen and Scarba

© Kilmartin House Museum

the differences between and similarities to examples further afield, and this gives us more data to work on, but not necessarily the answers to questions raised. These data continue to expand throughout Britain, and one day a new discovery will perhaps change our thinking about it.

Because rock art is part of our vast prehistoric heritage, our recording places an obligation on those who are legally responsible for it. There are threats to its safety, such as erosion or vandalism. In the past, ignorance has destroyed much of it, and what we have left is probably the tip of the iceberg. Like other countries, we are looking at each panel to assess not only threats to its existence, but are working out ways to preserve and display it. It is everyone's heritage, and we must have sensible access to large parts of it. If a panel is threatened in any way, steps have to be taken to protect it, often by covering it up. On reading this book I hope you come to share these interests, curiosities and concerns.

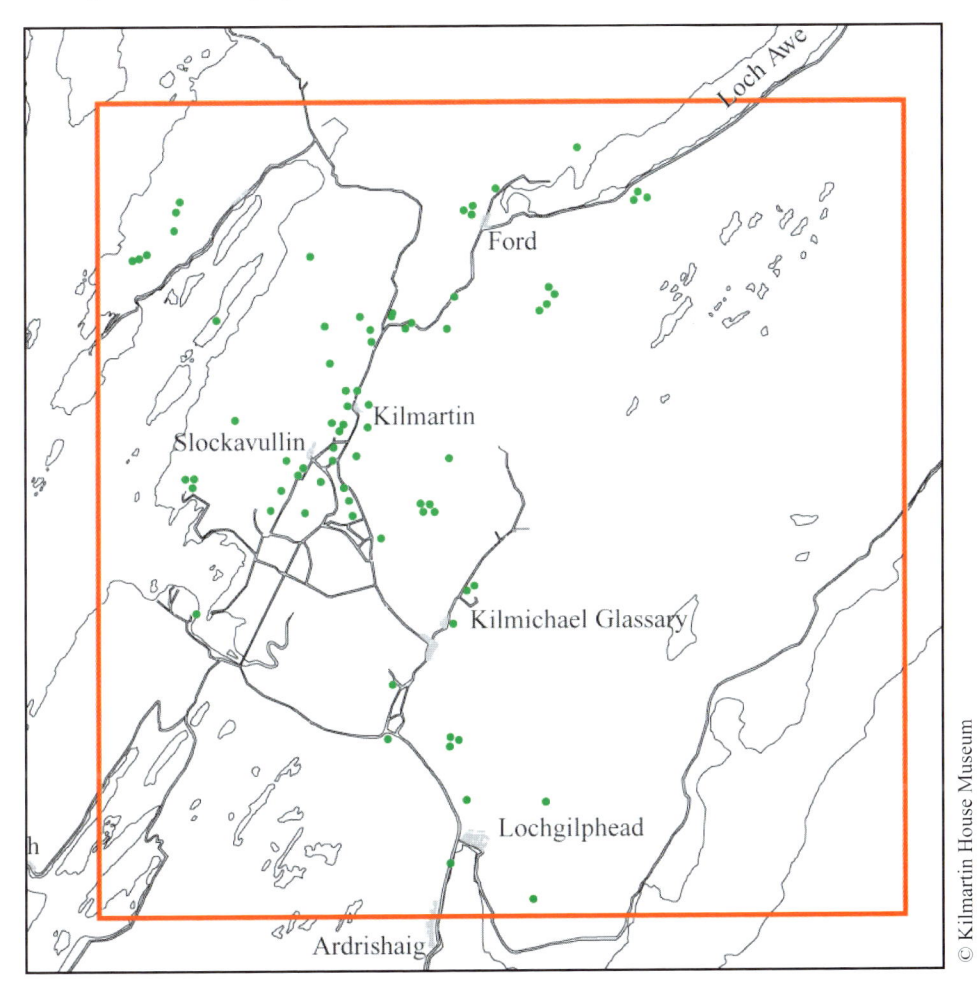

3. Area location and the distribution of marked rocks covered by the book.

Text and illustrations

Information about the sites comes either from new discoveries, or from literary sources, particularly the Proceedings of the Society of Antiquaries of Scotland. Wherever possible the 'history' of each rock is given. Most panels of rock art are described to enable readers to understand the arrangement of symbols with help from accompanying illustrations. To make this possible, a vocabulary has been used that is best explained in this diagram:

4. Main symbols and motifs

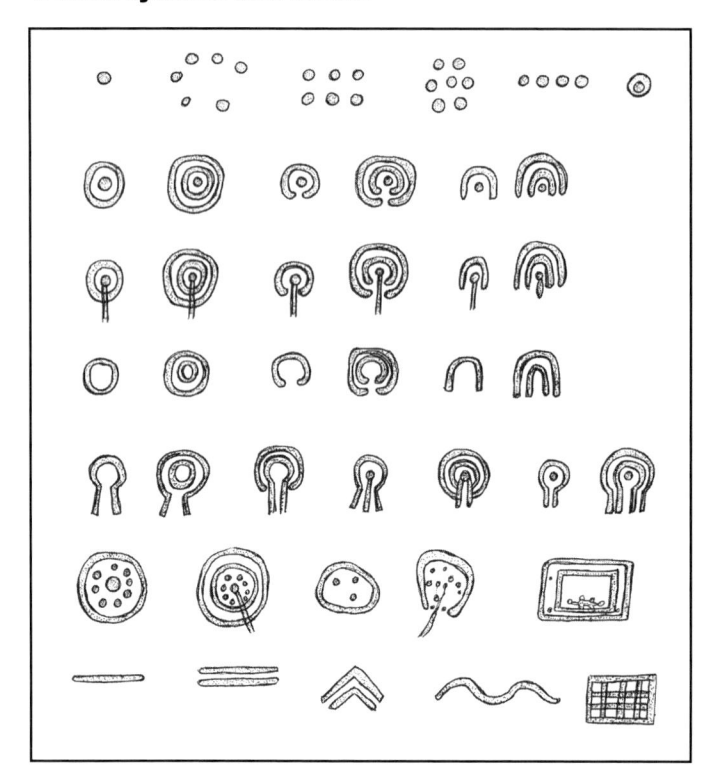

Line 1: Single, grouped cups and a countersunk cup.

Line 2: Cups without grooves at the centre of single and multiple rings, penannulars and arcs.

Line 3: Cups with grooves at the centre of single and multiple cups, penannulars and arcs.

Line 4: Single and multiple rings, penannulars and arcs.

Line 5: 'Keyhole' figures.

Line 6: Circular, oval, heart-shaped and rectangular grooves enclosing random and organised cup marks.

Line 7: Single lines and multiple chevrons, a serpentine groove and grid.

Drawings are based on rubbings, the details transferred to graph paper and checked against photographs taken on many different occasions. In future laser technology may do this, but it is expensive and not yet possible to record all rocks in this way. The photographs reproduced here are from slides, prints and digital images. Although landscapes are best captured on slide and print, digital photographs are particularly good for close-ups of detail, image-editing software enabling features to be enhanced. Location and mapping of sites are now much easier, thanks to the use of GPS (global positioning system) that is very accurate and enables people to find recorded rocks that may become covered over. All recent recording has used this system.

2. The lie of the land

Mid-Argyll is one of the most attractive parts of the British Isles because it is so varied. There are mountains, hills, wide and narrow valleys, streams, lochs and a superbly-indented west coast along which the islands are visible from the mainland. The number of sheltered gardens along the coast testifies to the warmth of the North Atlantic Drift current and its protection from the worst of the Atlantic weather by the islands. There are inlets that provide access to the land where the steep cliffs allow and afford passage to small boats to and from the mainland. Among the highlands are sheltered areas that allow some cultivation or pasture. Higher ground could serve as hunting areas or further pasture for prehistoric farmers; this was later to provide platforms for small defensive enclosures known as 'duns'.

Much inland ground is now forest-planted, especially a great swathe in the east and south east, and this has not allowed much archaeology to survive. It might not have been of much arable use in the past. Among the high ground ranges are lochs that would have provided vital fishing, communication by boat or raft, a path or a place to lie in wait for the animals and game birds that might feed at the water's edge. It was in such locations that primitive people left many traces of their lives.

At the centre of this varied landscape is the Moine Mhor, now a Nature Reserve, that has played such an important part in history. Here the River Add winds its way from its source in the north east down the glen to Kilmichael Glassary before making a U-bend north west to Dunadd, continuing its meandering way to the sea at Loch Crinan. To the south the artificial Crinan Canal marks the limit of our study area at north Knapdale.

5. The River Add at Dunadd

The River Add is fed by other streams, especially the Rhudle Burn that flows from Kilbride, and by the much longer Kilmartin Burn. The valleys so formed are linked to Loch Ederline and Loch Awe through a valley in which the small village of Ford is central, south of which is a watershed that determines that the Clachandubh Burn flows into Loch Ederline and not south west to the Kilmartin Burn. These streams and rivers mark the faults in the ranges that are generally aligned north east to south west, the direction of the main mountain-building movements.

This account of rock art takes in an outlying area to the east on the shores of Loch Fyne centred on Minard. To the south, burns reach the sea at Lochgilphead. Although there is some dramatic highland, with raised outcrops and cloud-capped peaks, there is a great deal of subtlety in the landscape, where just a slight rise in the ground can command a view of many miles of countryside. What is so difficult for us is to try to ignore today's vegetation and to imagine the scene over 4,000 years ago, when the climate was warmer. A very powerful statement about the rate of historical change is evident in Kilmartin Glen. It is hard for us to realise that much of what we see today – lines of cairns and standing stones – was once covered with peat, and that it was the cutting of that peat in recent times that exposed monuments at least 4000 years old.

6. Kilmartin: cairns, terraces, hills and Jura

Originally the rocks were sedimentary (sands and clays laid down by water) shales, limestones and sandstones, but huge mountain-building movements of the earth's crust transformed them, through heat and pressure, into quartzites, schists, phyllites and marbles. These are known as 'metamorphic' rocks because their forms have been changed. They are twisted, raised into ridges, thrown out of their original alignments and plunged into depressions or lochs. All have a north east-south west direction. Into this general trend, volcanic activity has forced other kinds of rocks. Great ice sheets then covered the whole area, flowing south west over what is now Loch Awe, deepening it, and Loch Fyne. As the ice retreated the land rose, exposing raised beaches along the coast, and the tidal flatlands of the Crinan Moss. After the ice came a warmer period when birch began to grow, and later oak, but this forest began to disappear, perhaps as it was chopped down by settlers who cultivated crops and raised stock. Climatic change certainly played a part in what followed: at the time of the rock motifs, the cairns and the standing stones, it was warmer and drier, but by about 2000 BC the weather worsened and rain soon caused the land to become boggy as peat began to form. Moss grew in layers to form bogs, blanket peat on high ground and on the wet flatlands. So it remained for thousands of years after the land had been abandoned, sealing in traces of settlements and monuments, until about 200 years ago, when peat-cutting revealed the lost civilization below. The challenge now is to discover where these prehistoric people lived, what they did for a living, and what they believed. Despite the abundance of monuments, finding their homes has proved difficult indeed. Peat-cutters could not miss piles of stones and standing stones, but traces of hut circles or wooden fences may not have been so obvious.

The relatively flat area from Kilmartin to the Crinan Canal is flanked in parts by raised terraces of sand and gravel left behind by ice sheets and floodwater. Sand and gravel-based soils are often easier to plough than heavy soil such as clay, and are generally better drained, so it is likely that the still-visible flat terraces have been good places to build houses and stockades and perhaps to provide fields for cultivation. The large number of monuments in the area suggests that the people living around them were successful in their colonisation, using the area for hundreds of years. It is interesting to note that in the high ground surrounding the valley and plain there are patches of soil that would have been used for small-scale farming too. A later sign of this land use is in small areas of rig and furrow ploughing for arable. Here raised strips that were drained by the furrows on either side increased the soil temperature slightly. They nestle in small hollows in the hills. What is very frustrating is the lack of evidence of settlement compared with the proliferation of standing stones and cairns.

7. Raised gravel terrace and quarry, Kilmartin

In stony areas, cairns are usual for the burial of the dead. The simplest, earliest forms in Britain are known as 'long cairns' or 'long barrows', depending on whether they are made of stone or earth, but there are all kinds of variations in design, including passage graves, chamber tombs and a local variant called Clyde Cairns. Basically, the construction is of a passage which leads into chambers that contain human bones. The whole structure is covered with stones picked off the fields or from streams, but slabs were used for the main construction work. Piling on loose stones also helped to clear fields for ploughing and for harvesting cereals and hay. The 'doorway' into the cairn could be at either end.

The Clyde Cairns that we see in the Kilmartin area contain burial chambers that are rectangles made of upright slabs that support large capstones. This box-like chamber could be divided into units by using overlapping side slabs supported by laying slabs across the box (these are known as 'septal stones'), and could enable the box to be enlarged. The chambers had roofing slabs resting on top of the uprights. So far, so good, but there is no simple plan, as tombs attracted later burials once they were established as important ritual centres. Thus an ancient tomb could be reused by inserting a cist (a stone chest) into it with a burial inside. This might be decorated with cup marks and axes of a much later period than the original cairn. The long cairn might then have stones heaped upon it to turn it into a round one. What we see on the outside

8. Nether Largie South chambered cairn

is the latest modification. Excavation pushes history further back to the beginning, if possible.

The other type of monument that emerges in our landscape from the peat-cutting is the standing stone, either single, in lines, or in a circle. Fortunately the Temple Wood circles have been excavated using modern methods and a sequence of over a thousand years has been revealed, including the discovery paralleled all over Britain that stones often replaced timber circles. It also established the changing use of that site, for one circle was closed off by adding horizontal stones, cist burials placed in the centre, and the interior filled with cobbles.

9. Nether Largie standing stones

This very brief account sets the scene for the main thrust of this book: how rock art fits into the total picture. It is already clear that we are dealing with only a partial picture: we see in part and we prophesy in part, for no matter how much archaeology has advanced since the discoveries and musings of the early antiquarians, there are questions to which we still have no answers. By examining the location of each decorated rock in its landscape and historical context, some new ideas about prehistory may be floated, pointing out what isn't known for certain and when there has to be speculation. Whatever the outcome, the sheer delight of exploring a beautiful part of Britain will be evident; something that can be shared with you.

3. An Overview of British Prehistoric Rock Art

Before giving details of rock art in the Kilmartin area, it may be useful to provide a more general view of the characteristics of British rock art. Markings were made by hammering designs into rocks with a hard stone tool, probably with the aid of a mallet. There have been recent experiments to make motifs on rocks: stone carver Andy McFetters, for example, pictured here at Kilmartin in May 2003, used a hard pointed stone as a hand pick (suitably protecting his palm with a leather pad) to make these designs in 12 hours. For a BBC TV programme, Ray Mears, working with the author on 'An Essential Guide to Rocks', used a similar technique with a hand-held pick of andesite on a soft sandstone block. Pick marks are especially visible when a rock is freshly uncovered, and even after a hundred years of exposure can remain individually visible. The basic symbols are known as 'cups and rings', with considerable variation that makes it unusual to find two designs exactly the same. Other motifs, including spirals, are an almost insignificant minority.

The quality and durability of the designs on rock depend to some extent on what the parent rock is. In Northumberland, which has one of the greatest concentrations of rock art in Britain, almost all are on sandstone. In Cumbria and Kilmartin, igneous and metamorphic rocks are much harder. It is not common for cups and rings to be smoothed out; usually the pick marks are left as they are, and originally the breaking of the surface of the parent rock might produce a different colour beneath. Cups tend to be an inverted cone-shape and quite shallow, and a careful examination reveals a rather frilly edge. Further examination shows how grooves are made, sometimes by joining a series of cups and picking out the gaps between them. Seldom are rings 'circular'; more usually they are angular. A design may be unfinished, as though the act of picking out symbols was in itself the important thing; one must guard against filling in the design by eye and not assume that erosion has removed part of it.

10. Andy McFetters

Generally a pattern follows the downward slope of a rock, as we see in the way in which ducts run from cups. The key thing to remember is that the whole surface was taken into account when markings were added to the surface, so that natural cracks, lumps, depressions and so on were incorporated in the design or suggested it. The direction in which a rock faces, and therefore the direction of sunlight that illuminates it is subsidiary to the shape and slope of the rock, and what can be seen from the rock is fundamental to its choice.

Not all the available rock surface may be used; sometimes the edges are left as a border. It is not always the best working surfaces that are chosen – quite the contrary in some cases – nor the highest outcrops. There may be many reasons for this; not all surfaces may have been uncovered and available, and there may have been reasons that are lost to us, never to be rediscovered.

11. Cairnbaan 2

Of particular interest is any sign of one design being imposed on another (a 'palimpsest'), for this can indicate a change of plan, a re-use, and a time gap between one phase of marking and another. Once all the designs in any area have been recorded, it is interesting to see whether similarities or differences occur there, and whether comparisons can be made with other parts of Britain. This does not mean that people necessarily copy each other's designs; it is equally likely that, with such a limited number of symbols available, people in one part of Britain could hit upon the same combination as another. The 'rosettes' that occur in Ormaig also occur in Northumberland, for example, but it does not follow that people had to have contact with each other to create that design. Spirals are common all over the world, without any connection being established among the people either in time or space.

Rock art occurs in four contexts: in the landscape, in burials, monuments and as portable examples.

12. Ormaig rosettes

Art in the landscape

In the landscape the late Neolithic/early Bronze Age people chose the best viewpoints and some special contexts such as stream sources. The markings seem to be associated with trails which nomadic pastoralists and hunters followed above valleys, not on the best agricultural soils. Had there been tree cover, some would have been in forest clearings, but many were on outcrops with little vegetation around them. Some could have recorded a special event, such as a feat of hunting or a death. We don't know.

Recent work (Bradley et al) has looked at the relationship between the complexity of images and their position in the landscape to identify if they were used for different audiences. Whereas there are many cases of more elaborate images being at the highest places (perhaps intended for visitors to the area), the simpler cups and single rings appeared on low ground for use by the people who lived there

13. Ben Lawers 1 (Loch Tay)

all the time. Like many theories, there are many exceptions, but it certainly works reasonably well in the Tay valley. There is enough material in the Kilmartin area to test the theory, but with caution: just because there are no multiple rings this does not make a design 'simple'. There are many sophisticated designs produced by arranging cups only into patterns.

There are many other things we don't know, despite new data. We cannot reach into the minds of people from thousands of years ago to understand how the symbols originated, how they were used or what they meant. It is possible that over a thousand years of use the people who used them had forgotten their origin; all they knew was that they meant something and that the marks had to be made. It is particularly difficult to understand what they meant in the landscape, but

14. Ben Lawers 2

we can say that the shape and surface of rocks were important to the designs, that the addition of motifs enhanced the rocks and their position in the landscape. We cannot date them from this, only speculate about the apparent nomadic element incorporated.

15. Chapel Stile

A recent discovery was made by Paul and Barbara Brown who, during a week's holiday in Cumbria, decided to look carefully at places where other discoveries indicated a logic behind the placing of motifs in the landscape. In the valley leading from Lake Windermere to the Pike o' Stickle (one of the most important quarries for the production of high-quality polished axes exported all over Britain) a massive block of andesite tuff was found to be covered with motifs that had not been reported (Chapel Stile. NY 3140 0582). This was a good example of putting theory into practice - which is how new sites are sometimes found (Beckensall 2002).

In Northumberland there is a particularly fine decorated rock shelter floor recorded recently at Ketley Crag (NU 0743 2978), but there were no traces of anything else, although rock art there does not occur in isolation, following the pattern of many sites where it occurs in clusters. The general site, called Chatton Park Hill has superb outcrop decoration and a decorated rock on outcrop inside a prehistoric defensive enclosure, presumably earlier than the fort (Beckensall 2003).

16. Ketley Crag

Burials

When we see the use of marked rocks in burials we come closer to establishing a time when they were used. Antiquarians noted the presence of marked rocks in graves, particularly inside the cists that housed burials of the early Bronze Age. However, some of these stones may have been decorated earlier and been brought in from elsewhere. The great chambered tombs of the Boyne Valley in Ireland are rich in motifs, both inside the chambers and passages and on the kerbstones, and of earlier date than the profuse clusters of later round barrows that are spread across Britain. That gives us an idea of the time span for the use of decorated stones in burials. Burials in mounds are one location for decorated rocks; in Northumberland there are decorated rock shelters/rock overhangs that contain burials – all late Neolithic/early Bronze Age in date, for cremated remains were placed in distinctive Food Vessels and Beakers.

Although there are several burials associated with rock art, their number is very small compared with the hundreds of round barrows recorded, so no general phenomenon can be established. Two excavated mounds in Northumberland at Weetwood Moor (NU 0215 2810) and Fowberry (NU 0197 2784), sites lying close together had been disturbed, the former three-quarters bulldozed. Neither had a cist nor any signs of burial. They lie in one of the most concentrated areas of rock-art in Britain; both incorporated decorated cobblestones that may have been carried to the site like wreaths to a funeral.

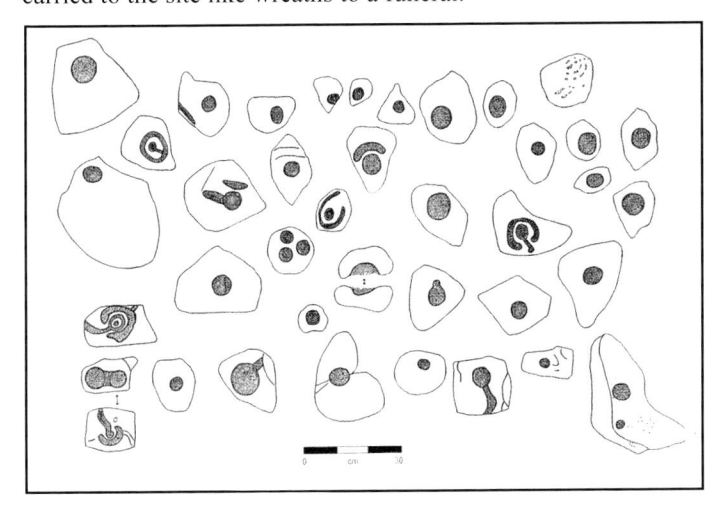

These cobbles (unquarried, partly rounded stones) would have been lying on the surface when the mounds were made, picked up, and the motifs pecked into them. All were fresh and showed no signs of erosion (Beckensall, 2001). The Fowberry mound was a double concentric circle of kerbs packed with smaller stones to form a low wall, retaining the rest of the mound of cobbles. It was built prominently on a 20m stretch of outcrop sandstone which was covered with a variety of symbols that took the natural surface of the rock into account.

17. Weetwood decorated cobbles

The Weetwood Moor cairn lay at the bottom of a plateau of outcrop that was covered with art; its largest stone, over 1m tall, originally faced inward so that its elaborate concentric rings around a cup and its three radial grooves would not have been seen. In the same cairn the decorated stones that survived the modern disturbance were face downward into the earth (Beckensall 2003).

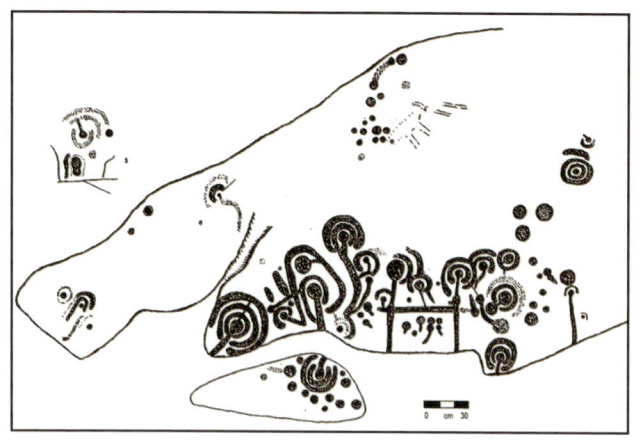

The occurrence of such stones in ritual cairns suggests a different use of rock-art, for the decoration was taken out of the open air where it looked to the sky and was buried so that no one could see it. If we assume that the mounds were not opened again for further use, it appears that offerings from the living to the dead were a private matter.

18. Fowberry mound

19. Nether Largie cist slab with cups and axes

Other cairns in Britain have similarly-incorporated decorated cobbles, some recorded and unexcavated; some have motifs within the burial cists. These tend to be in the cup and ring tradition, but in Kilmartin there are cists with metal-type axes as well. Here on one large cist slab (now displayed inside one of many large round cairns made of rounded cobbles) cup marks have been overlaid by pictures of metal axes.

The most important site excavated so far (but not published in full) was at Fulforth Farm, Witton Gilbert, near Durham, where a cist cover was decorated on the underside with cups and rings and the top with simple cups, some of them connected. Inside the cist were two pristine panels of rock art, every pick-mark visible, and the extended cist included cremations dated to c 2000BC. This means an extensive use of rock art over a thousand years, ignoring other discoveries on later sites where the rock art may have been introduced because of its tradition of ritual significance, or stone simply used as building material (Beckensall and Laurie 1998).

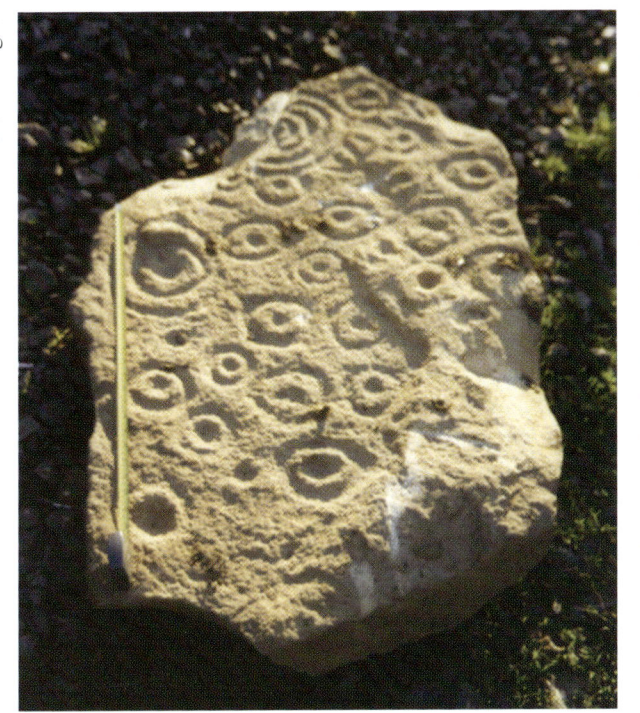

20 Fulforth Farm

An excavated rock shelter in Northumberland, a natural dome of rock that formed an overhang displayed a large circled basin and groove. On the floor of the rock shelter, which had been used centuries before by Mesolithic hunters, was a groove running down the floor to a triangular-shaped slab under which was a Food Vessel with a cremation (Corby's Crags, NU 1279 0962), (Beckensall 2001, 2003). At Goatscrag Hill (NT 976 371) in the same county a rock shelter with cups joined by curved grooves on top had Food Vessel Urns with many cremations buried in its floor. The rock art in this area leads along the top of an outcrop crag with decorated surfaces to the largest panel of decorated rock in northern England, at Roughting Linn (Beckensall 2003).

Although it is not possible to state categorically that rock art and burials in these cases were made at the same time, it does mean that the places chosen for both were significant points in the landscape. This occurs, too, with burial mounds that are built on other decorated outcrop rocks. More excavation might add to our knowledge. More and more discoveries are being made in northern England of cup marks, some with grooves, on or in cairns in cairn fields. Some of the cairns on which rock art occurs are likely to be much older than those at Durham, Weetwood and Fowberry. Here is one example.

At Old Parks (NY 5699 3988) in Cumbria in 1892 a large mound was demolished for road building. From pictures and accounts it was a long oval mound with a 4.4m spine of five standing slabs, three of them decorated with the beginnings of spirals (like walking-sticks) and rough enclosures, with all the pick marks showing that they had not been eroded. The mound was used for later burials: at least 32 cremations and examples of early Bronze Age pottery (Beckensall 2002).

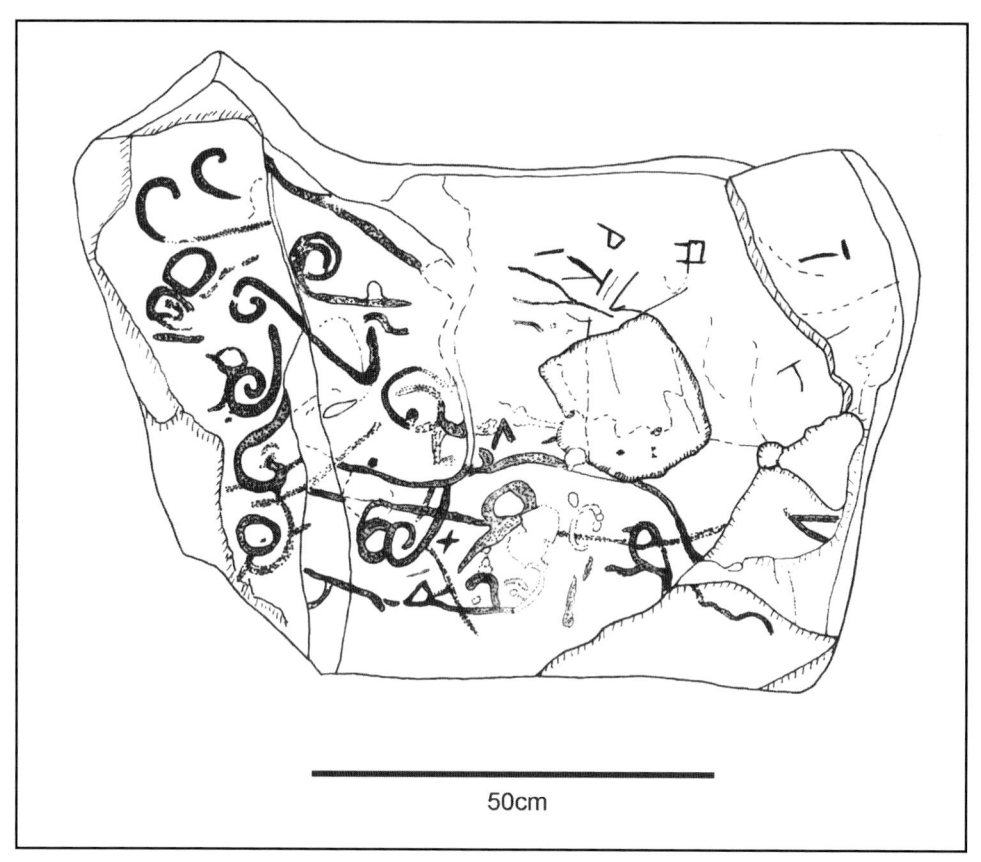

21. Old Parks

Art in monuments

There are many decorated standing stones in Britain, either single, parts of alignments or parts of stone circles. Rock art emphasises the importance of a particular part of a monument.

For example, the huge standing stone known as Long Meg (NY 571 372), Cumbria, covered with symbols, is the largest and only sandstone among igneous and metamorphic rocks. It lies outside the portal stones that lead into the circle, and may have existed there before the erection of the circle. The circle itself, though very large, is seen from aerial photography to be only one monument of many, for there are many ditches, one much larger than the stone circle, as part of a big ritual complex (Beckensall 2002).

22. Temple Wood

At Kilmartin, there are many cup marked standing stones that form a complex of alignments among lines of burial cairns. The Temple Wood stone circle (NR 826 978) has the advantage of being thoroughly excavated in recent times and reveals a thousand years' use. There are linked spirals on one standing stone, two concentric circles on another, and one of the horizontal stones that close the gap between standing stones has cup marks. An importantly-positioned stone at Castlerigg, Cumbria (NY 292 236), has recently revealed a spiral, and there are lozenge-shaped motifs on two others (Beckensall 2002). These examples, and many more, show that motifs from simple cup marks to more elaborate concentric circles and spirals played some significant part in monumental design.

Portable art

Portable rock art is on stones that have been moved from their original position by people; a term preferable to 'mobiliary'. There are hundreds of examples in Britain, with more being found each year; they turn up in spoil heaps, field clearance, rockeries, and are built into later structures such as souterrains, one in a kitchen wall and others in the foundations of bridges and castles. Many may have come from destroyed burial mounds; others have been quarried from outcrop. Some of the most interesting have been placed, perhaps deliberately, in later prehistoric structures, where, perhaps, their significance lingered on. The database for Britain is increasing at a satisfying pace, with new areas of the north being investigated. A major part of West Yorkshire has just been published, and the North Yorkshire Moors are revealing more rock art. We are also moving towards a more standardised policy for recording, examining the threats to rock art and considering how it should be displayed.

4. Setting the scene: Achnabreck

This book deals with rock art in geographic regions, but begins with one site that says more than any other rock outcrop about diversity of motifs and position in the landscape. It is also the largest decorated panel in Britain.

23. Achnabreck upper section

24. Detail: middle

The outcrop sheets of ice-smoothed metamorphic rock that provided prehistoric people with an extensive area on which to pick out their motifs were, until recently, in thick woodland, although the decorated sections themselves were in cleared areas. Now the whole site is open and accessible with car park, path, walkways, railings and notice boards. These allow visitors to view the surfaces without walking on them and damaging them.

There is a heavy concentration of motifs here, at one of the finest viewpoints. One may look south right down to the sea to Lochgilphead and to the west and north west to Cairnbaan. The two factors of a suitable surface and extensive views are satisfied. There are some more outcrops to the south below this site, remaining undecorated, and some scattered rock art in the vicinity. Above the outcrop is a possible cairn, and to the right of the path up to the site is a dun of a much later period than the markings. Although the views are spectacular today, what if the rock had been in woodland at the time the motifs were created? In that case the forest clearing would have held some great significance rather than the view – unlikely, but not impossible. Only core samples of the area around might answer that question.

The pristine outcrop surface already had some natural cracks and some scar lines where ice sheets had dragged stones across. The motif-makers took these surface features into consideration. The technical name for the type of rock is tremolite-chlorite-schist. There are two distinct outcrops that are close to each other. The first forms the westerly one that visitors encounter as they come up the path from the car park, the first markings encountered being on the lower slopes. In part these are steep, and, after rain, trickles of water continue to wet the rock long after the rain has ceased. A wet surface makes the motifs stand out, especially when a low sun adds its light to deepen shadows in the grooves. The best time to view them is when the sun is low in the sky: morning, evening or in winter. Overall, there are many cups, some of which cluster, are enclosed or at the centre of grooves. Many have a duct running from the central cup, down the slope. There are ringed enclosures and in the upper section there are horned spirals. In places the methods used to make them are revealed by pick marks. The smoother cups and grooves may be the result of water erosion. The rock surface is hard, and this leaves some clear edges. There are many variations on the cup and ring theme. It is not clear whether all the designs were made at the same time, and the fact that some are fainter than others may be because they were originally shallower, and some may not be finished. The western rock has its markings in three groups: lower, middle and upper.

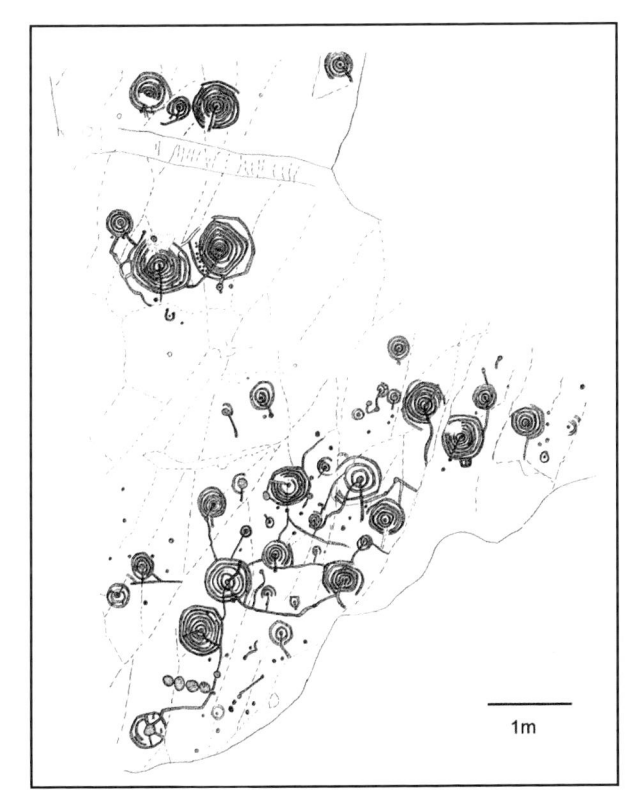

Lower group

This has the steepest slope, to the south. The most prevalent motif is that of a cup at the centre of concentric rings, with the cup acting as a centre for radial grooves and ducts that generally follow the rock downhill. Some unenclosed cups may have been on the rock before other features were added, some becoming incorporated in cup and ring motifs. There is a strong sense of flow and of inter-linked figures. Many are placed between natural cracks and some cracks are incorporated into motifs.

25. Achnabreck lower

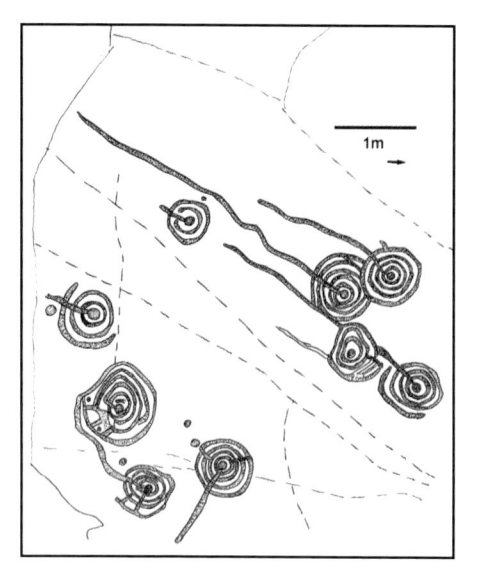

26. Lower Rock west

27. Achnabreck lower section

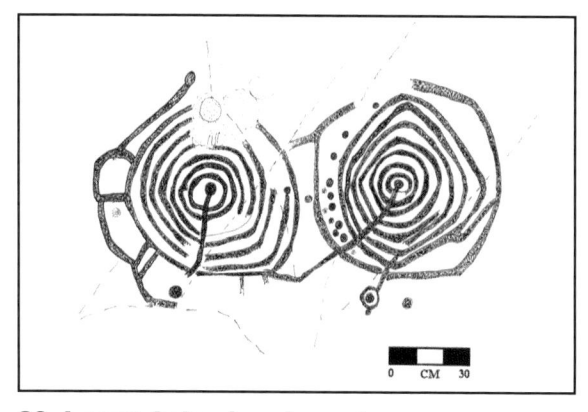

28. Lower Achnabreck west

At the bottom of the rock is a line of four large oval and round cups that are much deeper than the rest. In the middle there is a section bounded to the north by a natural scoured trough; this and a horizontal crack to the south enclose two of the most elaborate motifs. A cup at the centre of one has a duct leading down the rock. It is the focus of seven angular rings that are picked into the rock in short straight lines with rounded corners that give a general circular appearance. Between these and an outer ring that has a large circumference is a group of cup marks that either mark out an incomplete extra ring or act as a rosette pattern.

To the west another large figure has a cup and duct at the centre of concentric rings, but there are three conjoined enclosures added to the outer west ring. These two figures have much in common, and stand out from the rest. Further north up the slope there is a balanced group of three figures in line, cups with ducts at the centre of rings, the two larger figures balanced by a smaller one between them. To one side is something different: two cups surrounded by two concentric oval grooves (an 'occulus').

The most westerly group has three cup and ringed figures in a line; the largest at the centre has oval or pear-shaped grooves round a central cup, with the rings broken at one point by a series of enclosures formed by leading radial grooves out of an inner ring. This is linked to two figures on either side by grooves. Above them is a cup and four rings with the duct from the cup cutting horizontally across the rock – an unusual feature. At the north end there is a phenomenon that we see elsewhere (at Cairnbaan, for example) where one group of cup-centred rings cuts into another. From them very long ducts lead down the rock. Parallel to these ducts is another that runs from the outer ring of a motif linked by grooves to another above it. So this forms another cluster in which a distinct relationship is built up among motifs.

29. Detail of Achnabreck lower

Middle group

The rock outcrop here is less crowded, with a small scatter of motifs to the south and some very impressive, large figures to the north.

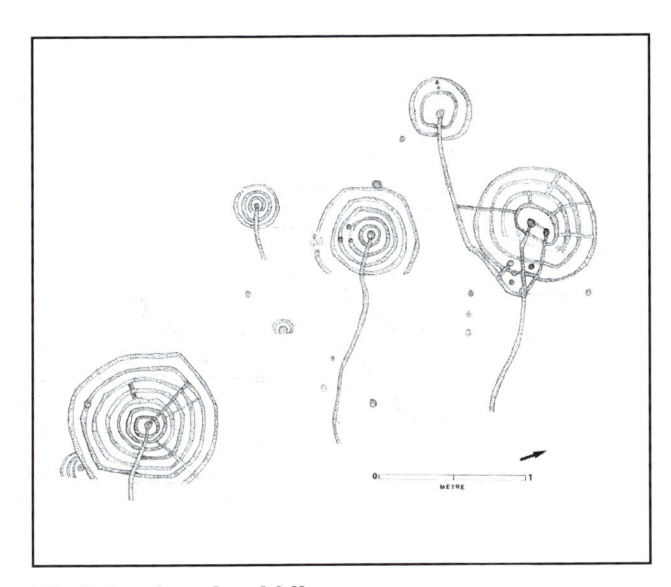

Here the rock slopes to the east, and long ducts that lead from central cups flow that way. At the centre are motifs where the rings are partly circular and partly angular, cutting through natural cracks, but stopping at a major crack to the east. The seven well-spaced rings are intersected by two deep radial grooves, a fainter one, and a groove that links only two rings. There is an additional figure of a cup and three arcs to the south that may have been added or was partly erased. Above this is a line of three figures increasing in size to the north, with the largest centred unusually on two cups with ducts leading from them to meet in a single duct that flows down the rock to the east. Again the concentric rings that began with an oval around two cups are well spaced (as at Poltalloch), they incorporate three (possibly earlier?) cups, and are cut through by partial radial lines. To the east where two ducts meet, a long duct from a cup that is the centre of two widely-spaced rings, meets at the same spot. A small 3-ringed motif to the south of these two is linked to them by natural cracks and by a possibly artificial groove.

30. Achnabreck middle group

Upper group

On the slightly sloping upper surface there are more variations on rock art themes. Furthest north is a rare horned spiral, its depth and clarity showing no signs of its being older than the others are. Beside it, picked to the same depth, is the more usual cup, duct and two rings. Both figures lie between two oblique cracks.

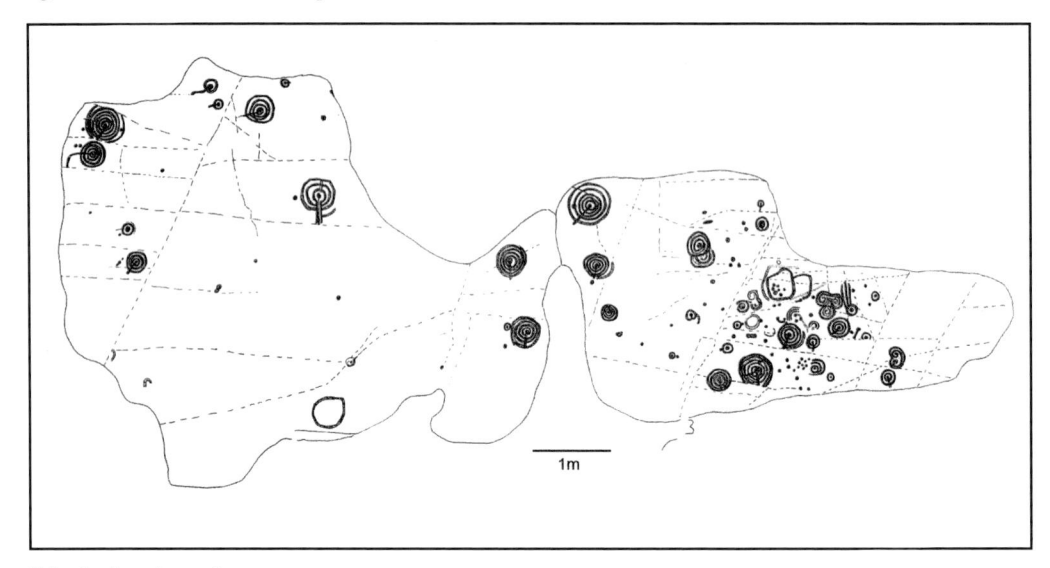

31. Achnabreck upper group

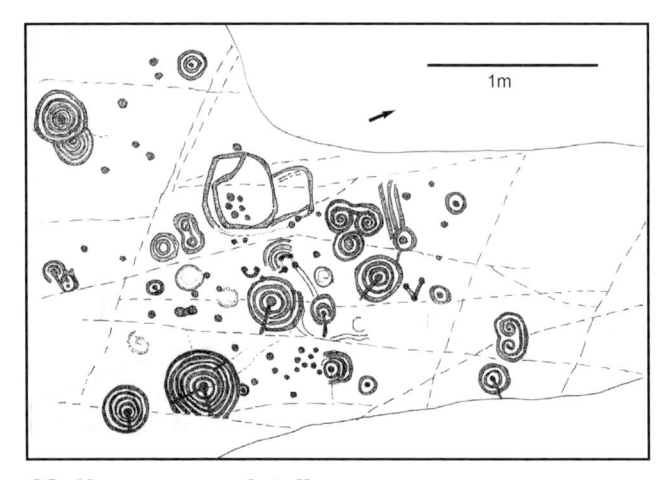

32. Upper group detail

In another space formed by large natural cracks and by smaller ones roughly at right angles, there is a concentration of variations that include a horned spiral linked to another spiral that forms a cloverleaf pattern. There is a fainter, similar design to the north of the crack, so we have three motifs based on spirals. Cup and ring design is splendidly expressed by a cup with two radials at the centre of 8 rings, five other smaller figures, and by cups and single rings.

There is a scatter of separate cups, an oval, a cluster, and cup clusters enclosed in a rough square with rounded corners, to which another enclosure adjoins. There are three parallel grooves that reach a cup and ring.

33. Upper group superimposition

34. Achnabreck Spiral Area

© Kilmartin House Museum

35. South end of upper group

The southern part of this rock has cups at the centre of rings, but there is a five-ringed figure that has been superimposed on a slightly smaller motif of the same kind. Towards the south end of the outcrop are two unique motifs: a ringed enclosure with nothing inside, and three well-spaced angular rings around a cup from which two parallel ducts emerge to the east and a radial groove to the west. This latter figure has an extra arc attached to the parallel ducts. To the south, (35) the motifs become more scattered and infrequent, but terminate with a fine cup and duct surrounded by five rings ending at a crack below which is a four-ringed motif, the duct flowing south from the central cup to join a groove leading out of another cup.

It is difficult to begin to isolate 'styles' in order to work out some sequence of events on this impressive rock. It is possible to group figures into categories like the number and spacing of rings, but this is a large repertoire that includes unique motifs and individual approaches to the arrangement of basic symbols into designs. That this rock could have been used for centuries may be likely but cannot be proved. Original analysis must be continually reviewed, for this can change the way we look at it. On every visit we may see something different.

The Eastern rock

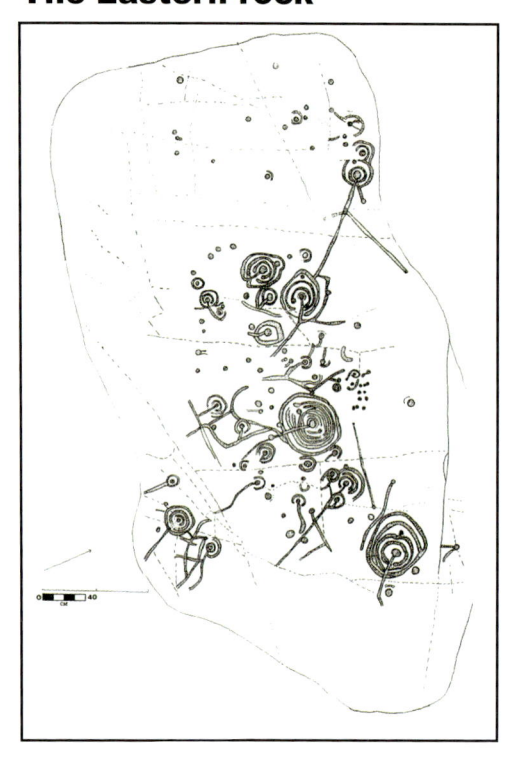

36. Achnabreck east

Detached from the rock surfaces just described, but part of the same outcrop a short distance away, the motifs here are limited to its top ridge and the south-facing slope. At the eastern end is a well-preserved motif with all its pick marks visible. Its central cup has a duct that curves to the east. Around it is a penannular, but the ring outside it dips slightly at the top to allow for a cup and a small duct. The next ring lies close to this second cup and from it emerges the north side of a fourth groove. The effect of this is to make the rings appear pear-shaped. An unconnected groove comes in from the east to run parallel to the outer groove of this motif. Two other motifs echo this design, when the outer groove is looped over the top of a cup. One of these motifs has an unusual angular attachment on its north side and is joined by a long duct running from a cup at the centre of two concentric rings. They lie in a crowded area of cups, some with single rings and arcs.

37. NE rock detail

At the centre of an apparent jumble of cups, rings and grooves is a series of angular rings around two cups. A duct emerges from one of them, to join with another parallel duct further down the slope from the outer ring.

The motifs appear more random than on the other rock, although it is noticeable that some uniformity is achieved because all the ducts flow in the same direction, determined by the slope of the rock. There are many scattered and clustered cups and a small 'occulus'. The south east corner has another variation: two grooves that divide two cup and ring motifs run parallel to those ducts that emerge from cups at the centre of rings, but have lines cut across them to form a grid.

Other sites

Another group of motifs is supposed to lie on an outcrop in pasture 140m SE of the large outcrop, but attempts to re-locate this have so far been unsuccessful. Ronald Morris recorded one cup and two possible rings, three cups with single rings, and a cup.

Recording

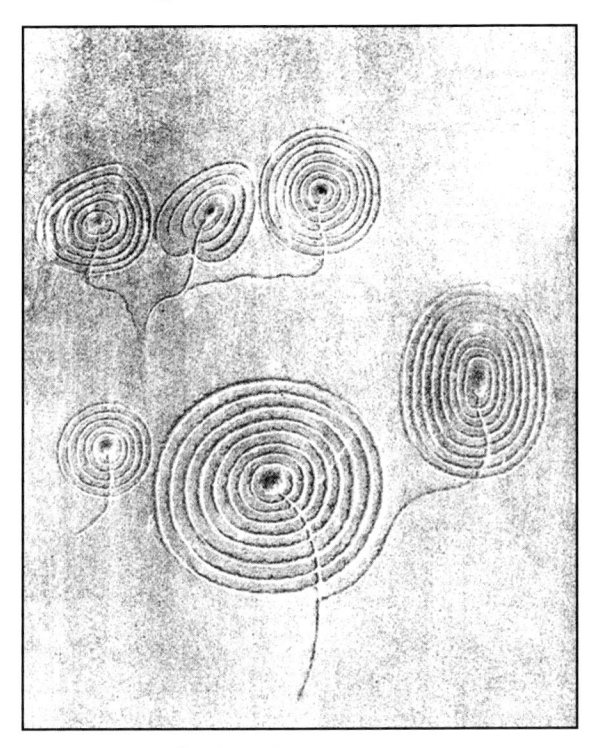

38. Simpson's drawing

The motifs were first recorded over 130 years ago by the tenant of the farm, Mr MacLean. They were referred to in numerous publications, including the famous *Archaic Sculpturings etc.* by Sir J.Y.Simpson in 1867, but it was not until Ronald Morris and his team got to work in 1970-71 that the rock was systematically recorded. A condition imposed by the Inspector of Ancient Monuments for Scotland was that no further turf be removed. The Inspector arranged for the removal of lichen and moss by 'three applications of non-toxic killer'. The recording system was a grid of rectangles 70x50cm, with white cord laid out on the rock. Each area was then photographed with a wide-angled lens and its number recorded.

Initially there were 500 photographs that provided a 'mosaic' on which to base the detailed drawings. Morris had help from university graduates, including Dr Elizabeth Shee, from Cork. He used a technique popular in Italy at the time: the motifs were roughly chalked in, then each section was covered with sheets of clear cellophane and the markings traced in black ink with a soft fibre pen. In cases of doubt, a rubbing was made of a specific motif. Once the drawing was complete and the chalk marks had been washed away by rain, the site was chalked again as a final check was made. The massive tracing sheets were photographed on a one-tenth scale.

Since then hundreds of photographs and rubbings have been made to check the accuracy of that report and subsequent recording by the RCAHMS, who cleaned the rock of all vegetation before their excellent photographic and drawing record. One problem in all recording is that on an irregular and sloping surface it is difficult to 'flatten' the whole thing out as a plan, especially over such large expanses of rock. It is possible that advancing technology, such as laser scanning, already tried out with success on other sites, will soon be applied to Achnabreck. Things are becoming easier to record, and more accurate, but the technology is still expensive.

Ronald Morris recorded 'at least 323 carvings – 183 cup marks unconnected with other designs, 135 cups and rings, 2 spirals, a few other designs and many radial and other long grooves'. He concluded that:

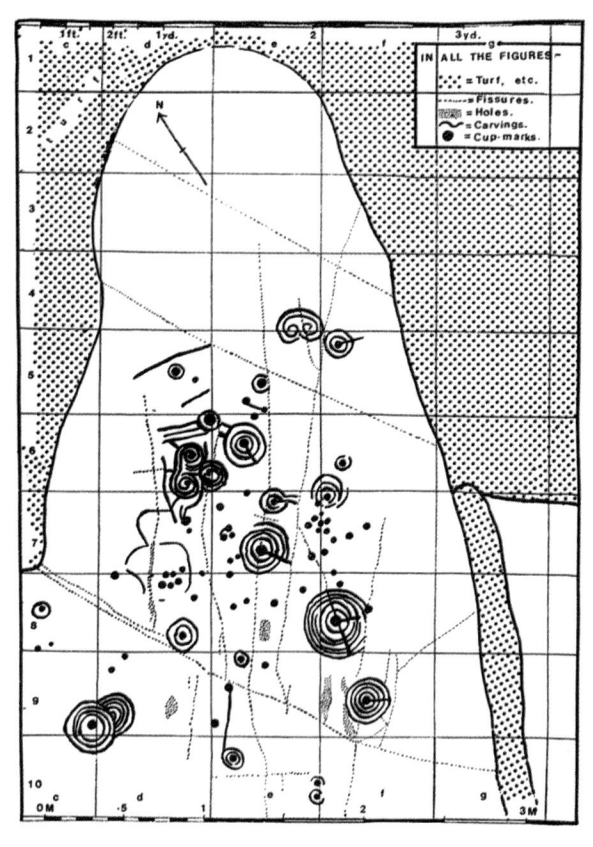

- all carvings with four or more concentric rings have at least one radial groove. So have most of the others, with the notable exception of the cups and one ring in the top area.
- as is normal in Scotland, the great majority of radial grooves run downhill. But, less usually, a great number of them are prolonged and connected with other carvings, grooves or fissures.
- as is normal in Scotland, most of the carvings are so sited as to be practically invisible in midsummer noonday sun, but to show up very well indeed in low midwinter sun.

39. Morris's drawing

A number of the carvings have been made to different depths, the cups being deepest. There is obviously much scope for further analysis by number-crushers. Some may have already spotted that there are three spirals and not two (Morris 1971.) Excavation accompanied the preparation and installation of the new walkways and other construction work, but no new motifs were found.

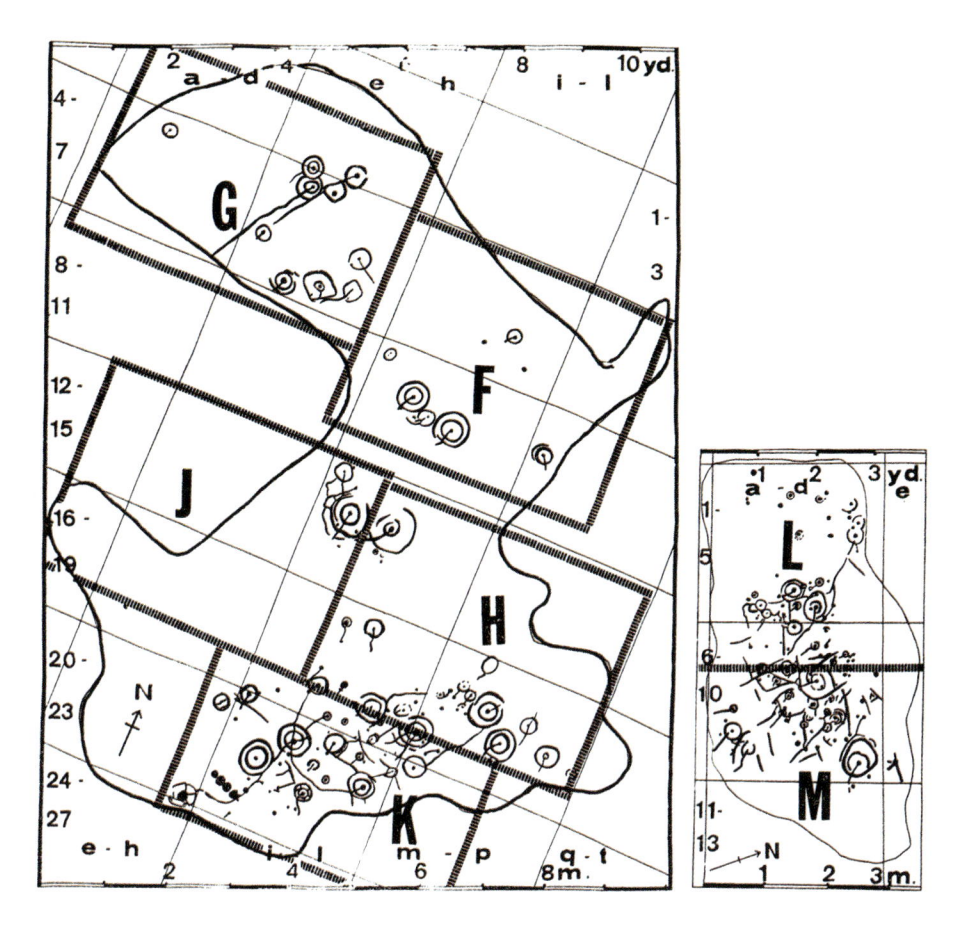

40. Morris's grid plan

There is a small cluster of marked rocks reported by Kaledon Naddair below and to the south of these. As I have not been able to record them in detail, they are omitted from this account.

5. From Lochgilphead to Dunamuck

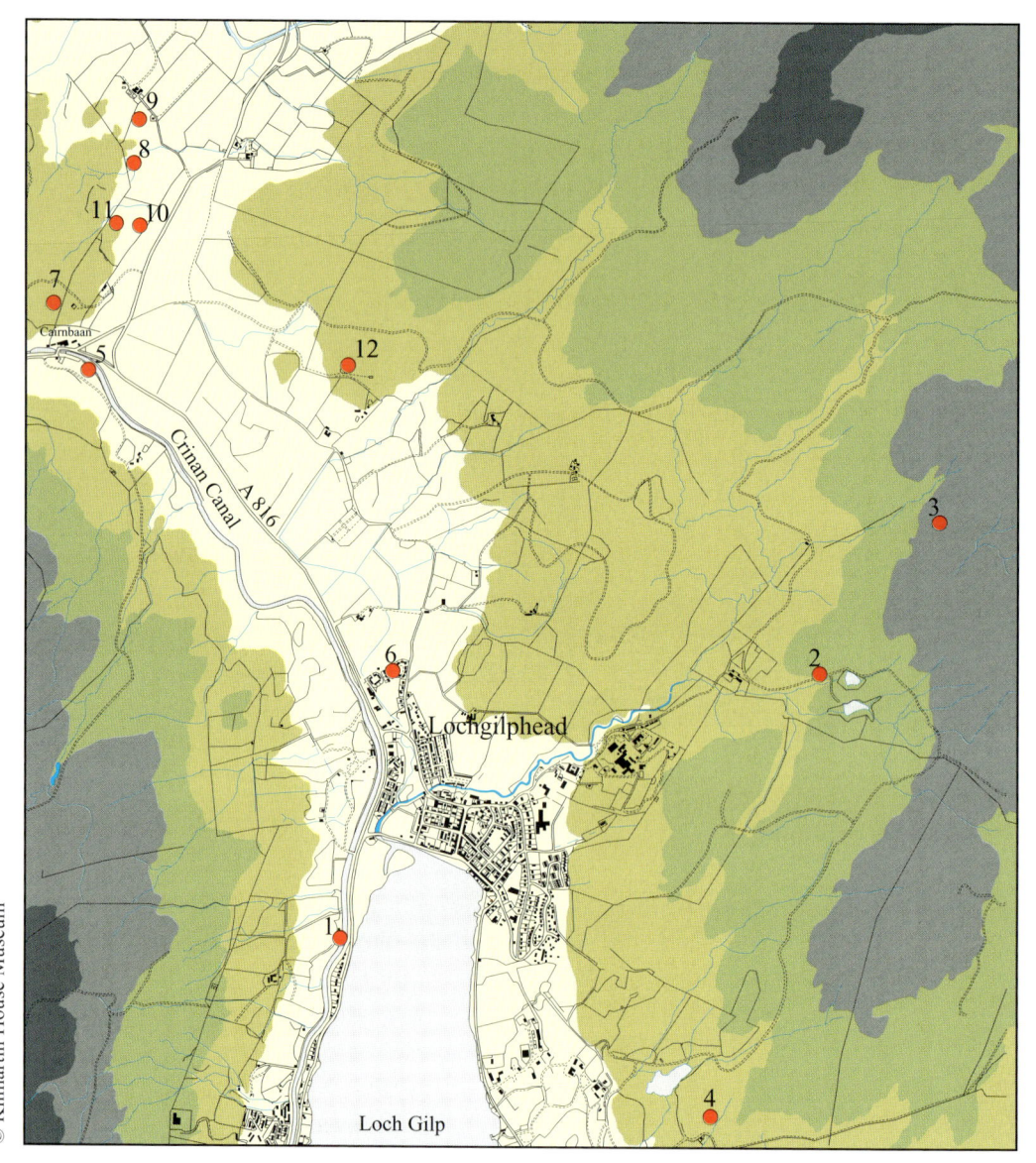

41. Site Location Map - Lochgilphead to Dunamuck

1. Torradh na Fienne
2. Blarbuie 1
3. Blarbuie 2
4. Dunmore
5. Carnbaan
6. Badden
7. Cairnbaan
8. Dunamuck
9. Dunamuck 2
10. Dunamuck 3
11. Dunamuck 4
12. Achnabreck

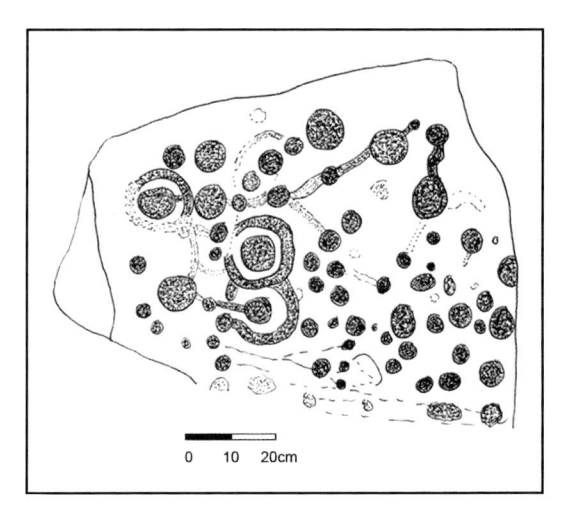

42. Torradh na Feinn (from a rubbing 2003)

© R. Morris

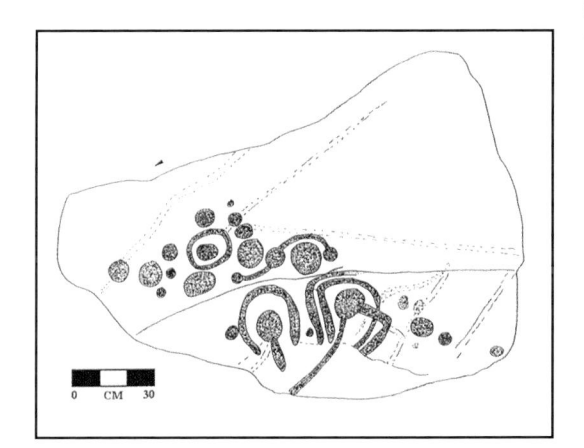

43. Torradh na Feinn

44. Blarbuie 1

Torradh Na Feinne
(NR 8554 8749)

A slab erected as a standing stone was found by Mr Duncan McArthur in his garden (now called and signposted as Brackley). First reported in 1970 by J. Davies, the schist slab was found half buried in his garden overlooking the sea. No investigation has established its original function, but the fact that the decoration covers the whole slab and none has been cut off makes it a likely cist cover. The decoration consists mainly of cup marks, single rings and some connecting grooves. This decoration continues just below soil level where one flat side of the rock has been laid as a base.

Blarbuie

1. Dermid MacGregor, a retired forester, helped to locate a slab hidden in a wood at NR 8830 8900, near to a forest track. It is an impressive slab disturbed by heavy forestry ploughs, and may be a cist cover. Marion Campbell recorded it (Campbell 1964), but no one had seen it since then. The motifs follow the natural configuration of the slab, which is divided lengthways by a ridge. Two figures with penannulars are set into the ridge, using the hollow to fit the curve of their rings. Some of the

cups are large, deep and symmetrical. One has a complete ring; two others are divided by an S-shaped groove marked by three small cups. Variety is achieved in a simple way. There is no record of any illustration of this site - the RCAHMS survey failed to locate it, and it does not appear in Morris.

45. Blarbuie 1

2. There is an outcrop in a well-grown plantation that is now extremely difficult to access. Paul and Barbara Brown and I rediscovered this (NR 890 898) and recorded the motifs on slide and with digital photography. We did not make an accurate drawing on our first visit in 2000. The design is very impressive, but previous recordings of a small spiral did not fit what we recorded. One photograph that appeared in print had the negative reversed. It was discovered initially by Marion Campbell, and was mentioned by Morris in 1971.

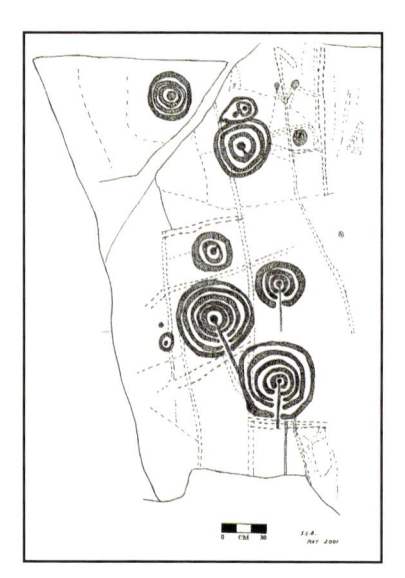

47. Blarbuie 2

46. Blarbuie 2

A full recording was made in May, 2001. Others had visited recently, and left behind a yellow bucket, white lavatory brush, and some small orange plastic markers in the trees. The site lies in the middle of a mature forest plantation, where the rock art is confined to a slab of outcrop that has a small cave-like opening underneath it. The place is a threshold where high ground is broken in a kind of pass, marked by a flat outcrop which rises to the north in a series of steps.

The motifs are not at the highest point of the outcrop. The use of the flat surface takes into account natural fine fissures and cracks, some of them mineral-impregnated, that run roughly from north to south. Other cracks, some apparently ice-scoured, run from east to west. The surface used by the motifs is generally even and smooth, but the north east part is more uneven. This has led to the false assumption that one of the motifs is a spiral: it isn't. Grooves from cups at the centre of rings follow the natural north-south cracks in the rocks, and some of the designs fit into spaces created between them and the east-west lines.

Description:

The motif on a westerly triangular section of rock, defined by natural cracks, is a cup at the centre of three rings. To the east there is a cup and ring, the cup linked to the ring by a short groove. It lies on the most uneven part of the rock surface, through which a major north-south mineral vein runs. Two cups on either side of this are linked by a V-shaped groove. A cup at the centre of three well-spaced concentric rings is linked by a groove to the inner ring. Superimposed on the outer groove is an irregular figure of a cup at the centre of an angular groove that is completed by four small joined pick marks. This and a cup is enclosed by an irregular groove that comes to a point at a major north-south crack that runs the whole length of the rock. The motif is later than the penannular motifs that it cuts.

Further south is a cup at the centre of two concentric rings joined to the inner ring by a small groove. Three figures to the south have a design of concentric penannulars around a cup from which a thin groove runs. The north east motif has four penannulars; the others have five. The lowest is to some extent made by using the natural groove, for this is the most angular penannular on its western edge. It is joined to the north west motif from the central cup.

48. Blarbuie 2 - detail

To the west is a cup and small ring, and a cup. Of great interest is the way the most southerly figure is related to the rock edge and its overhang. The groove from its central cup does not reach the edge, but running parallel to it from the outer penannular are two natural grooves that have been artificially enhanced. Further west is a slab that has two faint motifs: a large cup and four pick marks almost enclosed by a thin angular groove. Below this are three faint concentric arcs and a cup.

The position of this panel has a special place in the landscape rather than a general all-round viewpoint. It lies on a low position on the ridge at a convenient crossing place, but the small overhang suggests that something else is going on. The natural lines of the rock are directed at this edge from the north: the artificial grooves follow this direction. It is possible that the overhang, like a cave or rock shelter, had a special significance. As far as we know it has not been disturbed, and may contain something of interest.

The rock is in a good state of preservation. We cleaned it with brushes and water in order to record it, and this enabled us to make a more accurate drawing than others before us. After the recording (including many prints, digital and slide photographs) we re-covered it with vegetation to preserve it. There is a case for removing some of the tree cover over it so that in future others will be able to find and view it more easily, although the roughness of the forest area will continue to deter many.

Dunmore, Kilmory (NR 876 865)

A boulder was recorded near to Lochgilphead by Marion Campbell (Campbell 1964) below the fort on the south side. We located this, a small flat boulder with three cups joined by a straight groove that runs off at an angle to the edge of the stone.

Carn Ban (NR 840 907)

Motifs in a context are always of special importance - if relationships with monument construction exist, approximate dates for their inclusion may be considered. Lying south of the Crinan Canal the cairn is built on a rock outcrop knoll, merging with it at its edges. It was excavated some time before 1867 and is about 8m diameter and 2m high. It has a central cist built on the natural rock, and its capstone has an unusual *incised* design made up of lines that make use of a crack. There is a cup near its centre.

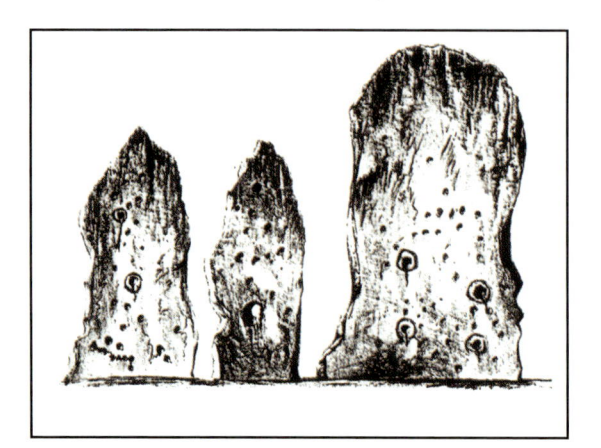

49. Lithographs by Collingwood Bruce, commissioned by the Duke of Northumberland, including Carn Ban (right)

Another slab of schist (Craignish phyllite) was found inside as a loose panel resting against the western side slab. It has multiple lozenge motifs pecked on it, and can be seen at the Royal Museum, Edinburgh.

The decoration is similar to that on the Badden cist and is not in the cup and ring tradition. It echoes some of the patterns on Beaker pottery, for example – lines rather than curves. At the centre is a pocked lozenge that has four others around it and the beginnings of a fifth. Across these runs a natural fault that divides the lozenge and slightly confuses the pattern. At the bottom left of the drawing another linear motif joins it; the block seems to have been split off at the base, removing the rest of the design. This indicates that the motifs were already on the rock before it was split off and put into the cist. In a sense it represents the removal of one respected monument and its incorporation within another (Bradley 2003).

The slab may have been lying somewhere else and put into the cist for its ritual significance. This happened in Galloway, at Cairnholy cairn. A cist in this chambered tomb had a slab decorated with cups and rings inserted into it. The cist cover had similar cups and rings, heavily eroded, on the top (Beckensall 1999).

Badden (NR 858 890)

Another site of a cairn in this region was found to the SE close to what is now the Crinan Canal, 400m SW of Badden Farm, and 1km NNW of Lochilphead. It came to light during ploughing in 1960, and the marked rock is now in Glasgow Art Gallery and Museum. On the site there were boulders that may have come from a destroyed cairn, some charcoal and a scatter of worked flint, but the interpretation of these finds was inconclusive. It may have been a settlement or a burial site, or both, at the SE end of a former freshwater loch that reached Cairnbaan before the Crinan Canal was constructed.

50. Badden cist slab (1.53m long)

At the top left-hand corner (SW) on projecting rock split by a crack are two cups in line, one with a duct that has three concentric arcs. Below in the next zone are cup and ring, a cup, long duct and a penannular. The main group of motifs occupies a long thin triangular area formed by cracks – a cup and two rings, a cup and penannular with a natural ice-formed groove following the long ducts from the cup, an oval enclosure with two cups from which grooves begin and end at a crack. This 'occulus' is similar to one at Kilmichael Glassary. To the right of it (N) is a complex group of cups: two with arcs, one with a duct, three linked that have a curving, enclosing groove around them. Other cups are scattered to the NE. There is a large cup joined by a groove to a smaller one, two cups with ducts and two small linked cups.

52. Cairnbaan 1

The lowest panel has a similar arrangement. There are six parallel grooves moving to earth from cups, some with single rings. The lowest motif is a large cup and small duct. The type of natural surface and the choice of motifs make this very similar to Kilmichael Glassary, to the extent that it is strongly possible that the same people made the motifs. Within the railings other patches of motifs are visible – cups, and cups with double rings.

It is quite surprising that only 100m further up the slope is a panel of outcrop decorated in a completely different way, more like some of the more elaborate markings at Achnabreck. Here the cracks are widely spaced, leaving large areas of the schist (pitted with small vesicles) that form distinctive panels.

53. Cairnbaan 1 - outlier

54. Cairnbaan 2, looking SE

55. Cairnbaan 2, NW

The outcrop, flush with the ground, is often wet even in dry weather. This is a possible spring source. The design gives an overall sense of zoning and fluidity, with most of the motifs linked together or running into each other. The natural cracks run SW-NE, forming zones that the groups of motifs respect. The designs were made to be viewed from the SE, as the ducts run in that direction, although the flatness of the surface throws the motifs into relief when the sun shines, so that they can be easily appreciated from many directions.

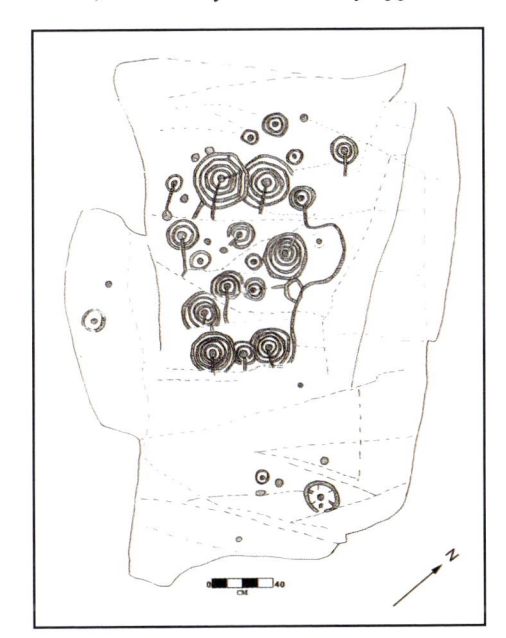

56. Cairnbaan 2

The top (NW) section has three cup and ringed figures in a row. The cup and four-ringed motif to the left has been superimposed on the three-ringed figure with an incomplete outer ring: this can be seen in the way the outer angular ring runs over the outer ring of its neighbour. Both cups have ducts, and an additional groove runs from the outer circle to the crack. The third motif to the right is smaller: a cup at the centre of two rings. Just above it to the right is a cup and duct with two rings and at the top of the rock is a cup and two-ringed motif. A line of cups near the left edge has two that end with ducts and, like all the others close to the crack, these ducts end there.

There are four more motifs clustered in the middle section, sandwiched between two major cracks. The motifs are almost all multiple concentric rings around a cup, with only three unattached small cups. The group of three is repeated at the bottom of the section, with two outer concentric circle motifs superimposed on the smaller central cup, duct, and two rings. The larger figures have four or five rings. Again, all the ducts flow to the SE. Another group of three is immediately above, all connected by their outer rings. The largest figure at the top of the section is a cup and four rings without gaps, and although cracks form its outer ring, they are artificially enhanced. Five more cup and ring motifs complete this group, one with its cup and duct leading to another cup. One has two cups; the other four have one.

The lower section has three cups, one ringed, There is also a cup at the centre of a ring with possible eroded radiating grooves that begin at the cup and end at the ring – an echo of Poltalloch. There is an attached piece of outcrop on the left side that has a cup and ring, and a cup and duct.

The site was first reported by Sir James Simpson in 1864, and has since figured frequently in literature. There has been some speculation about a 'fish' motif in the area, and Ronald Morris thought that this might be on the lower outcrop. 'Disregarding a few grooves which do not fit the pattern, some of these grooves seem to form a giant 'fish' about 3.5m x 0.75 m.'

Dunamuck

With the permission of the farmer, three of us explored the land to the south of the lane leading up to the farm. On the opposite side of the lane are the remains of a very large cairn. The most important part of our recording was on a sloping outcrop ridge that has wide views over the cairn towards Kilmichael Glassary, but not the main Kilmartin valley. The valley from this outcrop ridge includes standing stones, giving the area a ritual significance. The rock art is a very recent discovery, and was not known by Morris and Campbell. This record is new and previously unpublished.

57. Dunamuck outcrop

The outcrop sheet, **Dunamuck 1** (NR 8433 9180), is a smooth, close-grained metamorphosed sandstone, light brown in colour. The motifs are clearly but lightly pecked, no attempt having been made to deepen them. The upper surface of the rock is exposed, with motifs visible, and a little of the thin grass cover at the base was rolled back for recording and replaced at once. At the top of the slope is a deeper, matted grass left undisturbed. The distribution of motifs is spread lengthways, with the grooves from cups and rings following the natural downward slope of the rock. Natural cracks have been incorporated in the pecking of the motifs.

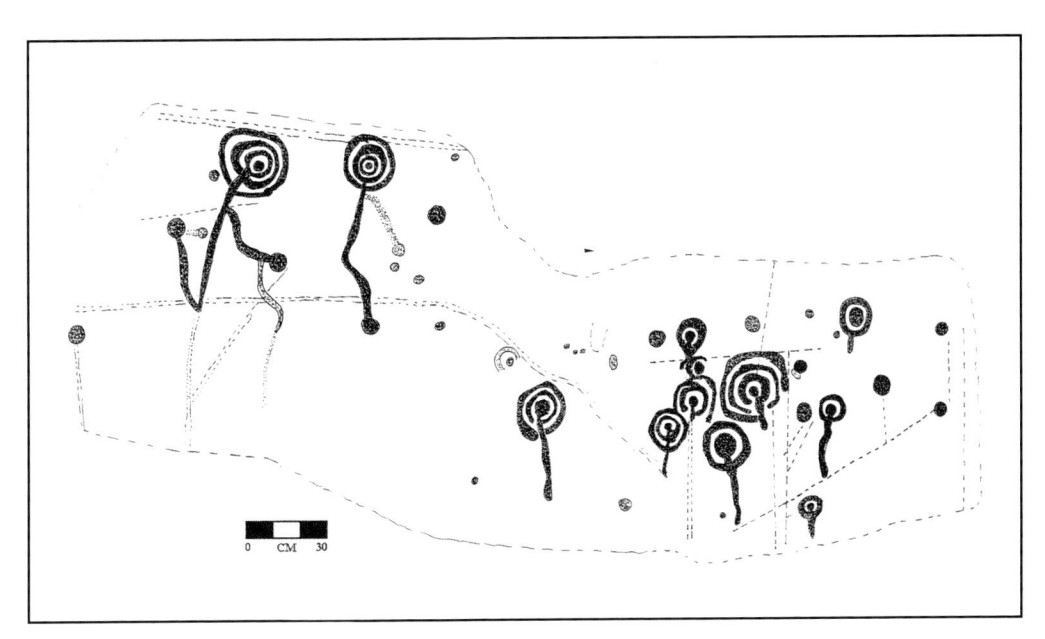

58. Dunamuck outcrop: east-facing outcrop

Detail

What determines the placing of the motifs appears to be the cracks from west to east, directing the grooves from cups at the centre of concentric rings. There is a scatter of cups, but the main emphasis is on cup and ring motifs. To the south on the upper slope is a cup with three well-spaced concentric rings, the outer of which incorporates a small cup. These rings are somewhat angular. The inner ring marks the start of a groove that follows the line of a crack down the slope. A well-made cup is linked to the bottom of this groove with a pecked, curved groove. To the north a curved groove links to another cup, with another curved groove branching from it. To the south of the concentric rings is a cup.

A similar cup and ringed figure lies to the north at the same level, less angular and more circular, with three rings, a groove running down the slope from the second ring. A rough radiate groove runs from the inner circle up the rock to the outer circle. Again, the groove down the rock begins to follow the natural crack line, then curves away to join a cup. A fainter groove branches off to another cup in a similar way. There are five detached cups to the north of this figure.

The second group of motifs is arranged lower down the rock to the north. Here again the dominant feature is a number of cups at the centre of between one and three rings, with grooves leading from their centres down the rock. The southerly figure in this group is a little detached from the rest, a cup and groove with two penannulars. The others are boxed in by natural grooves that run vertically down the rock, the largest figure being three concentric rings around a cup with a very short groove. The outer ring is incomplete, allowing the crack to continue

59. Dunamuck 1

its course. Another motif of two penannulars around a cup uses a crack to extend a vertical groove down the rock from its central cup. Here four motifs impinge on each other. Below the three-ringed motif is a well-made large cup at the centre of a single ring pierced only by the groove from the cup. The northern part has four well-made cups and two smaller ones. The highest motif is a cup with surrounding ring from which a short groove emerges.

Below is a similar motif, with a long, curving groove leading from the cup. The lowest figure, which shows every pick mark in its construction, has its groove parallel to all the others, running from a cup in a single ring.

Dunamuck 2 (NR 8439 9209)

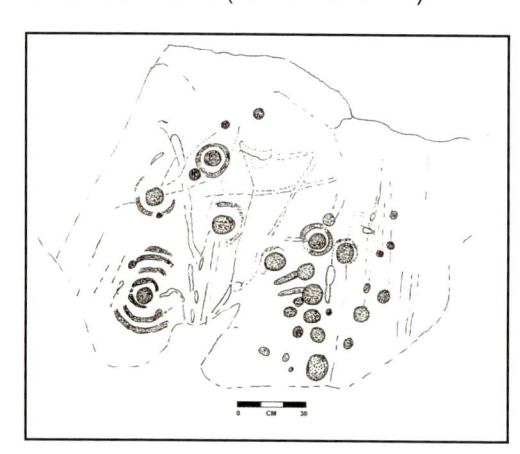

60. Dunamuck 2

To the north, near the farm road, still within the field bounded to the west by a wall and a wood, and near to the cottage, is a vertically-set outcrop whose upper surfaces between cracks are marked with cups, some with rings. The top surface is scarred with parallel grooves from glacial action. It is not an easy working surface, and this may account for the incompleteness of some of the man-made grooves.

The largest motif is a cup with four concentric, incomplete rings. Six other large cups have single rings that are either not complete or very faint. There is a row of five large cups, two of which have grooves leading from them in the same direction, and they are accompanied by other smaller cups. Some cups are pecked into the striations, some faintly and others more distinctly. Given that this outcrop is not an ideal surface for marking, its choice may have depended on its dominant position in the landscape, calling for extra recognition. The use of large cups points to a connection with the site at Kilmichael Glassary.

Dunamuck 3 (NR 8440 9154)
At the south end of this outcrop is a spring that becomes a small stream, and is joined by others. In the valley below is a single cup on a flat slab that stands on a raised part of the valley.

Dunamuck 4 (NR 8424 9151)
This slightly domed outcrop close to a modern track has a cup and cup and ring. The rest is mostly covered with turf.

61. Dunamuck 2

Dunamuck 5 (NR 843 914)
The site is a rise in pasture caused by the outcrop that has extensive all-round views of the landscape.

Most of its surface is usually grass-covered, with only a little of the rock visible. There are many close, parallel fine cracks on the surface that run roughly from north to south. Over and among them are cups, some large. Some are at the centre of 1-4 concentric rings and one at the centre of two penannulars. One ring is distinctly square with rounded corners. One cup has a faint broken ring.

62. Dunamuck 5 and 6

The general impression is of motifs arranged in lines running down the rock slope, especially emphasised by a line of cups in the central area.

One particularly large cup at the top of the rock has two small pointed grooves like ears. The cup is connected by a natural groove to a cup and ring above it without a gap.

63. Dunamuck 5

64. Dunamuck 5

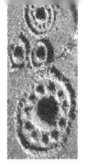

Dunamuck 6 (NR 842 915)

On detached outcrop are three large cups in a row, one at the centre of a ring of which the middle cup forms part.

Contexts

Below the rock art panels on a low hill overlooking the River Add valley are two cairns. One (NR 845 919) is about 33metres in diameter and 2m high, its outline changed by the dumping of field clearance (which often happens to monuments). The only features noted are two slabs at right angles that may be the remains of a burial chamber. No excavation has been done to check this. There are two other mounds that have been hit by ploughing near to the fallen standing stones. One is 19m diameter and the other 8m.

There is a reference in 1862 to three large cairns. In an adjacent field three circles and cairns were reported as having been blow up with gunpowder – also the fate of rock art at Poltalloch to make a path. Today there is nothing to be seen, but these snippets of information suggest an area of ritual activity similar to that at Ballymeanoch.

There are three groups of standing stones on the low ground beside the River Add leading into the valley and on to two others at Dunadd. Three stones in one group (NR 847 929), the central one fallen, are about 750m from Dunamuck Farm. The second group (NR 848 924) has two stones, and seems to form an avenue with the group of three to the west. A third group (NR 848 923), closer to the farm has two fallen stones. None of these has traces of cups and rings, but the decorated outcrops rise above them and over them. It is as though the decoration provides a window through which to view the ritual area below.

Below the Dunamuck sites the River Add flows in from the NE at Bridgend, near the sites at Kilmichael Glassary and Torbhlaran, which are situated in a narrow fertile valley suitable today for arable farming. The valley includes two standing stones, one of which is decorated. Where the river turns NW to the widening valley that leads to Dunadd, later to be the seat of Scottish kings, the route is marked by more standing stones at Dunamuck. A narrower valley that takes the modern road from Kilmartin to Lochgilphead branches to the SW, overlooked by the Cairnbaan site to the west.

6. The Upper Add Glen

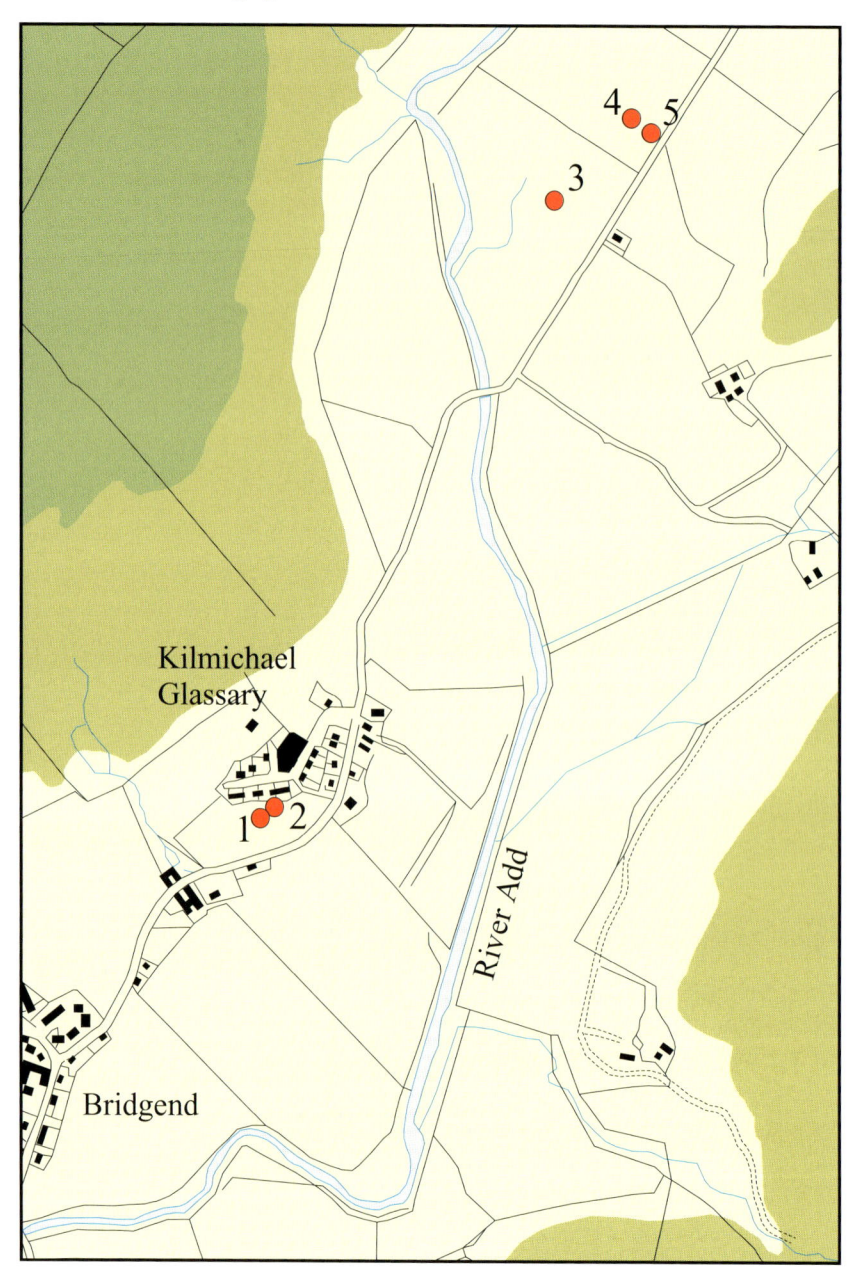

65. Site Locations in the Upper Add

1. & 2. Kilmichael Glassary
3. Torbhlaran 1
4. Torbhlaran 2
5. Torbhlaran Standing Stone

Kilmichael Glassary (NR 857 934 and 858 935)

The village lies on a slight slope extending from the north to overlook the River Add. The rock art lies just above the village in rough pasture that rises to high craggy outcrops. The main panel has railings to protect it, but the other remains open. There is a contrast between the motifs on the two outcrops, as there is at Cairnbaan.

66. Kilmichael Glassary: view from the site

67. Kilmichael Glassary 1 from the south

The long outcrop dips SE in two parallel terraces. The dominant motif is the cup, varying in depth and diameter, symmetrically made. These cups are arranged in lines following the closely-packed striations in the rock that give it the effect of having been combed very finely horizontally. A few cracks that run down-slope are widely spaced. The unmarked SE part that descends to the road is rounded where it dips down.

The upper part has a profusion of cups of many sizes. At the top one cup has a ring to which a small enclosure is added. Another has a keyhole-shaped enclosure. Below is a large cup with a thin penannular groove that ends in two cups. Running in line with the cracks are cups that are extended by adding other cups in a line and smoothing them into round-ended grooves. Many of the small cups here are paired, either touching or linked. Two have a long duct running south. A cup at the bottom has an arc. The lower outcrop sheet has its motifs clustered below those just described, leaving a similar sized area to the NE free of markings.

There are two more keyhole enclosures and a cup, and cup and ring. The lowest section consists of an irregular line of large well-rounded cups, those to the right incorporating grooves that run from the cups down the slope and others that run from arcs over the cups – all parallel.

69. Kilmichael Glassary large and conjoined cups.

68. Kilmichael Glassary lower east motifs

The lowest arrangement of motifs to the right is a long curving groove that begins as a ring around a large cup with a long duct, arches over a number of other motifs and runs to a crack. Within the enclosure thus formed is a small oval enclosure with three cups inside and an attached cup and ring. Two cups are joined by a groove. A cup and duct to the left is enclosed by an extended groove. The distinctive motifs in this enclosure occupy a space between two horizontal cracks.

There are seven cups arranged parallel to the cracks at the top of the outcrop. There is more rock art on an extension of this outcrop beyond the NW angle; 47 cups and 5 cups with single rings have been recorded, but these are not always visible. There is a possibility that more lie hidden. Located just north of a garden fence in untidy ground there is part of an outcrop visible that bears different kinds of markings from those just described. Superimposed on two cups at the centre of rings is a motif with five rings arranged around a large cup that has a short and a long duct running from it. The outer ring ends with a cup that may have already been on the rock. To the right (N) of the motif is a large cup at the centre of three rings that end at the rock edge. Above is a large cup with two rings, and a small cup with a gapped ring. Other motifs are cups, one ringed with its duct running NW up the rock. There is a row of cups at the bottom edge, above which is a small rectangular enclosure that is linked to a cup and natural cracks, making the largest figure look even more complex.

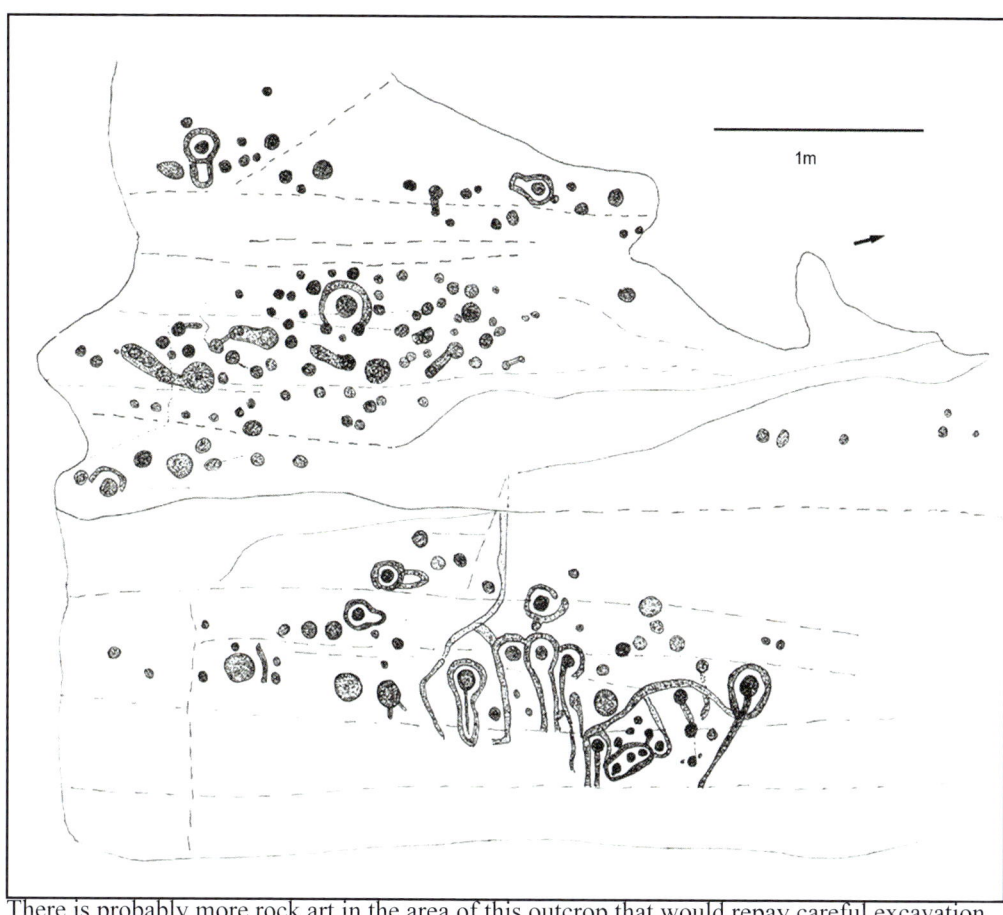

There is probably more rock art in the area of this outcrop that would repay careful excavation.
70. Kilmichael Glassary

71. This picture shows how long grooves were made by joining cups.

72. The northern motifs: a photograph taken at the time of discovery.

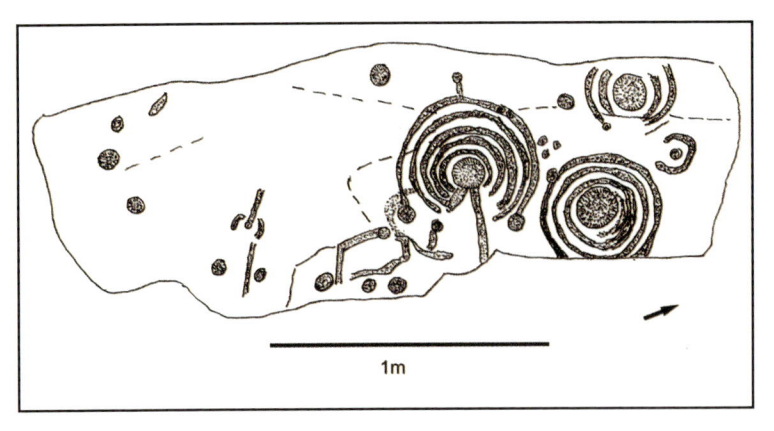

73. Northern motifs at Kilmichael Glassary

Torbhlaran
(NR 863 945 and 862 943)
Within the Add valley is an isolated outcrop ridge that stands above the field, running SW-NE. To the east on a spur are three cups with

74. Torbhlaran outcrops

single rings, a cup and four rings, and three cups. On the west spur is a cup and ring. In the middle are three cups and a faint cup and ring, and 190m SW of the above is a whale-backed outcrop running SW-NE that has widely-spaced cracks. Marion Campbell first reported this site in 1960. At the SW end is a small group of six cups, one with an arc. Further right are two cups. The main group consists of cups with between one and three rings, and many cup clusters, some in line and some touching. The ringed motifs include two that have a duct running from a cup at the centre of three rings. The one to the left incorporates a cup in its outer ring and is linked to a cup and two rings by a fine groove flowing from the cup. Other ringed motifs are gapped but only two have a duct running from the cup. However, some of the motifs are so faint that it is not clear whether parts have been defaced by erosion. Exceptionally good light conditions are needed to view all the details on the rock. Part of it has been blasted by quarrying. This outcrop was first reported by B. Thomson in 1969.

The Torbhlaran standing stone (NR 863 944)

This standing stone lies in a field NW of the road from Kilmichael Glassary to Ederline. It has a flat top, slanting sides and two flat surfaces on the SW and NE. The SW face has a concentration of about 30 cups from its lower third to the buried base. These appear to have been arranged in oblique lines, but could be random. There are nine cups on the NE face. Another possible standing stone has been used as a bridge over a ditch, 570m to the SW.

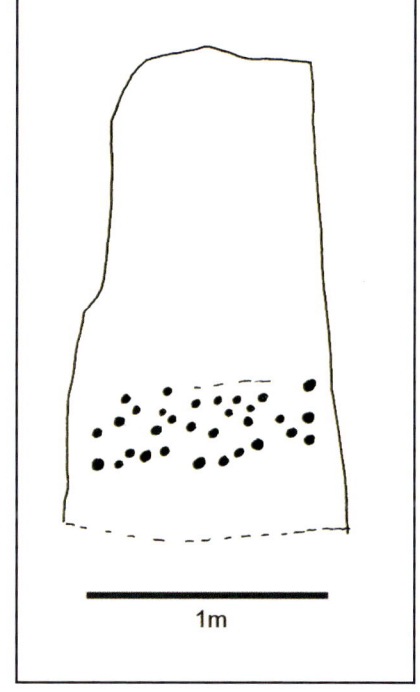

75. & 76. Torbhlaran standing stone

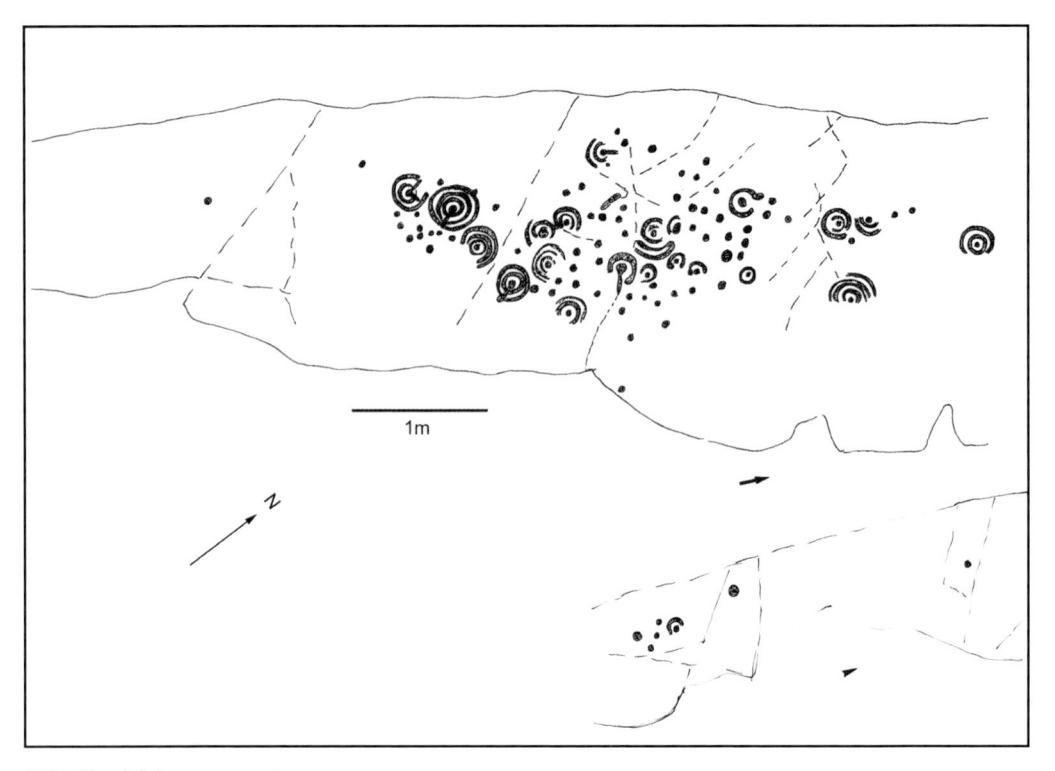

77. Torbhlaran outcrop

7. The fringes and central area of Kilmartin Glen

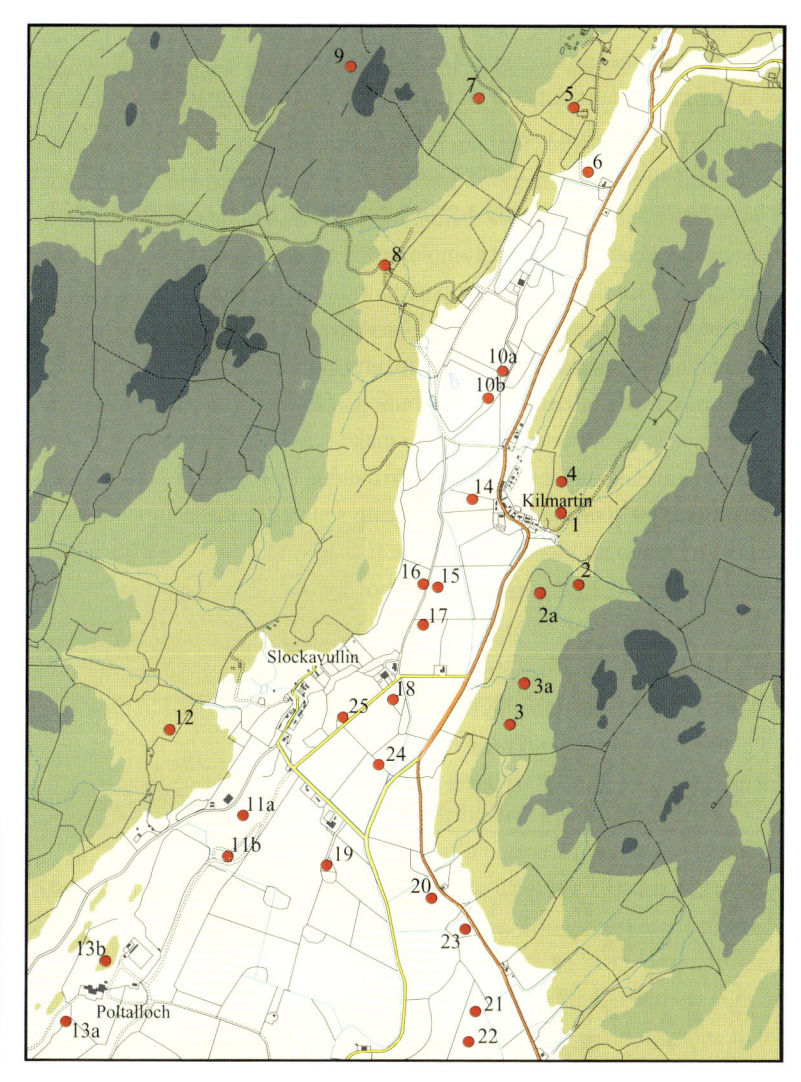

78. The fringes and central area of Kilmartin Glen

1. Kilmartin 1 2. Kilmartin 2 2a Kilmartin 4 3. Kilmartin 3 3a. Kilmartin 5
4. Kilmartin Castle 5. Carnasserie Castle 6. Carnasserie Cottage 7. Carnasserie Standing Stone 8. Glenmoine 9. Meall a Braithain 10a. & 10b. Upper Largie
11a & 11b North Poltalloch 12. Ballygowan 13a & 13b South Poltalloch
14. The Glebe Cairn 15. Nether Largie North Cairn
16. Nether Largie Decorated Rock 17. Nether Largie Mid Cairn
18. Nether Largie South Chambered Cairn 19. Ri Cruin 20. Baluachraig
21. Ballymeanoch Henge 22. Ballymeanoch Cairn and Stones 23. Dunchraigaig
24. Nether Largie Standing Stones 25. Temple Wood

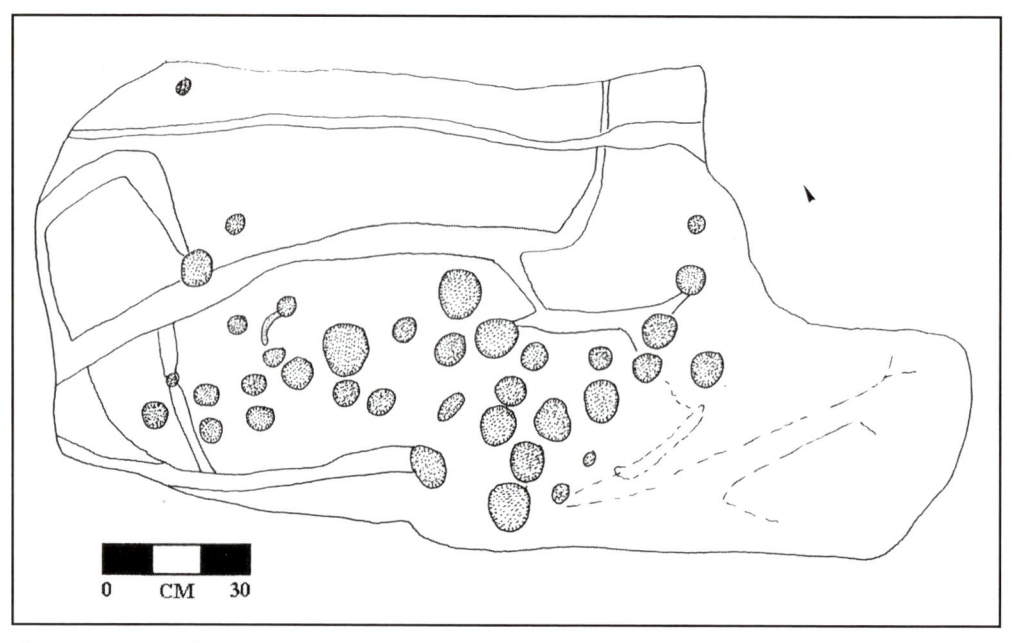

82. Kilmartin 2

The glen reaches its highest point to the south before dropping steeply southwards to the ritual site at Baluachraig, close to the marked outcrop there (NR 831 969). In the southern part of this narrow glen, in an area that has at least two systems of narrow rig and furrow ploughing or cord rig, now grassed over, lies a fairly even-topped boulder **Kilmartin 3,** (NR 835 977) that has 22 cup marks, one of which is countersunk. There are low enclosure walls that cross the glen. Springs are stream sources on the high slopes to the east, and the area would have been well watered. The whole territory needs a thorough survey to establish the nature of its use, but significantly the land has been used for cultivation and pasture, rendering it potentially capable of sustaining a hunting and pastoral community.

83. Kilmartin 3

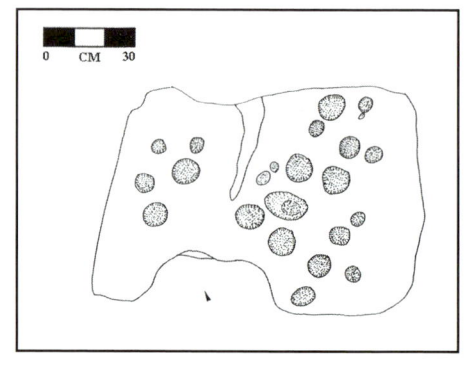

84. Kilmartin 3

60

In 2002-3 two further decorated boulders were discovered in the same area, again by Paul and Barbara Brown, **Kilmartin 4** (2a on the map) with cups and single rings and **Kilmartin 5** (3a on the map) with paired cups.

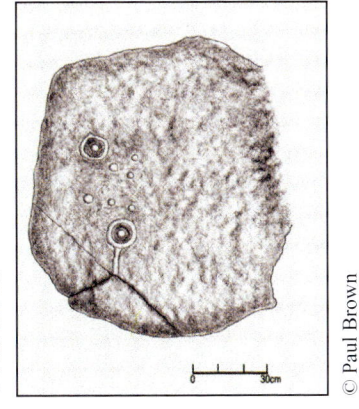

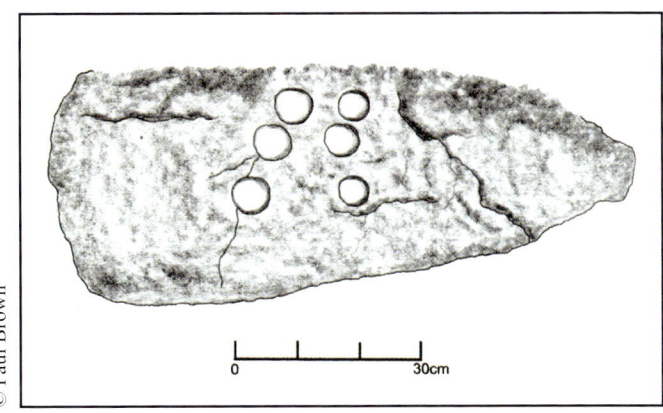

85. Kilmartin 4   **86. Kilmartin 5**

It is significant that all the new rock art panels are not outcrop, but boulders; that they lie at the same altitude as the more complex rock art such as Cairnbaan, and above the complex art at Baluachraig. Height above sea level does not determine in all cases whether the art should be complex or simple; a more important reason for the simple art at this location is may have been its status as a working area rather than at a concentration of monuments.

We followed the route of a track from the high ground to the plain below, where the complex rock art of Baluachraig lies and the monuments that include cairns, standing stones and a henge. It was clearly a very important ritual centre, and we have concluded that this route is probably ancient.

87. Above Kilmartin to the gravel terrace

At NR 836 991 a cup marked rock lying on the 100m contour was reported 30m SE of Kilmartin Castle (4 on the map). This 'single faint cup can be found overlooking the village on a flat needle-like outcrop pointing SW' (DES 1993). On the opposite side of the glen the gravel terrace has been partly excavated in advance of new gravel extraction, and some prehistoric discoveries made there at NR 832 993. The interim article that describes it is entitled *Prehistoric ritual and funerary complex* (Ferry 1997).

A major discovery was a 46m-diameter timber circle and other features, understood to be ritual and funerary. The site is a platform of outwash gravel on which the timber circle was erected. Inside was a sub-rectangular enclosure, part of a palisade trench and a ring of posts around a pit. Leading to it from the south was an avenue earlier than the timber circle, and two cists. The excavator's conclusion was that the earliest activity may have been a 'cursus' perhaps associated with the post ring and pit. Once the excavation of the timber circle and the sub-rectangular enclosure was completed, nothing conclusive was learned about the latter. No dates were available. One cist contained a burial, fragments of pottery and some possible flakes. This was very disappointing to those who expected a site in such a significant area to have produced more.

Ahead of gravel extraction, 3 cists were revealed, one with a Beaker at its base, at NR 832 993 (DES 1993). The site lies on an important route through the glen that can be followed south as a public footpath initially in the direction of Poltalloch. Other minor rock art discoveries in the area are:

88. Carnasserie Castle

Carnassarie Castle (NM 838 008)

9m west of the NW angle of the castle is a slab with seven cups, five of which have been cut through, perhaps from outcrop.

Carnassarie cottage (NM 839 004)

A rectangular block of stone lies north of the track to the castle, 20m west of the cottage. There are two cups with pick markings visible.

Carnassarie standing stone (NM 834 007)

Marion Campbell reported that the northerly standing stone has a cup 0.008m in diameter and 0.013m deep, 0.61m from the base and 0.53m from the south edge (Campbell. 1964 PSAS 95). Close to the main glen, but leading away into the higher ground of the north west is Glenmoine.

Glenmoine, Upper Largie (NM 828 000).

A track that leads from Kilmartin past the gravel workings up the hill reaches an abandoned farm with a sheep fank behind it. Our recording of a boulder 5m west of the NW wall of the field is drawn from a rubbing. The rock is very difficult to find in thick vegetation.

89. Glenmoine location

The rock has 26 cup marks. Two of these are linked by a groove. Two cups with single rings are joined from the centre of one cup to the ring of the other. One cup is countersunk and another has a faint ring. Closer to the glen are minor discoveries at Upper Largie. It would not be surprising if more were found in this area, as it is a classic site overlooking Kilmartin Glen from a slightly higher ridge, an extension of the glacial terrace.

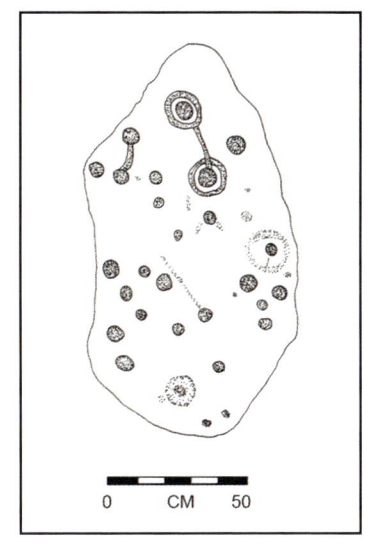

90. Glenmoine

Meall a'Bhraithain (NM 826 010)

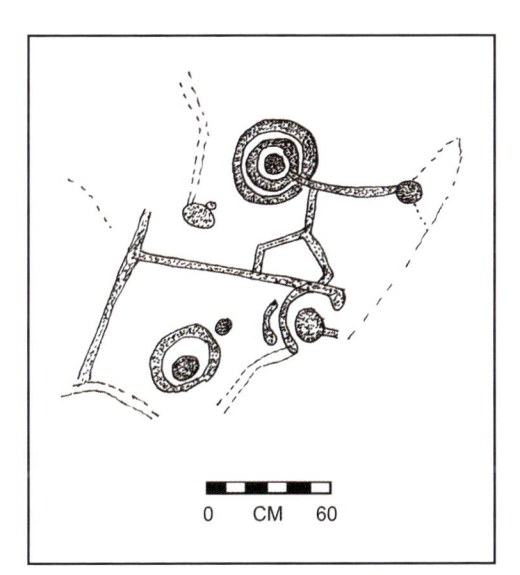

91. Meall a'Bhraithean
Sketch based on R. Morris

The site, NNW of Glenmoine is now difficult, if not impossible, to find as it lies in forest. Marion Campbell (1961) described it as a sheet of outcrop 1.52m square on a saddle between two hillocks on the 182m contour, with several small cups and a central group of three cup and rings 'joined by meandering gutters suggesting stylised figures'. We have not been able to locate these, but Ronald Morris did (1977). He gives a photograph of the markings and a chalked-in photograph alongside it (Arg. 64, page 107) that confirm Miss Campbell's description. He adds that the gritstone rock is smooth on top and has a cup and complete ring, one with a radial groove from the cup, and another has a cup and incomplete second ring. In addition to the connecting angular grooves (some of which may be cracks) there are four cups.

It lies among glacial mounds on the west escarpment of the main watershed ridge, NW of a hillock with twisting projecting rocks and SE of a ruined dyke, overlooking the top of Ormaig glen.

Upper Largie (NR 834 994)

On smooth outcrop there is a panel with four cups, four possible grooves, one crude cup with an oval gapped ring and cup running from it, and two cups with gapped rings, one with a short duct (DES 50, 1994). Nearby is a rock with four cups.

Upper Largie (NR 835 995)

In a rough grass field NE of the first house on the track is a long outcrop ridge with a cup and complete ring on a horizontal panel (DES 1993). It is very likely that there will be more found in this area, as it extends from the glacial terrace north and overlooks the glen from a low height.

Slockavullin

The modern linear spread of houses that makes up Slockavullin has every appearance of once being an important site, overlooking as it does some of the most imposing monuments in Kilmartin Glen. An ancient track from the north passes through this settlement. Much of the housing may have covered significant sites, but at the north end is a large outcrop ridge that Naddair exposed and found to be festooned with cups and cups and rings. These are no longer visible, having been reburied.

Leaving the principal monuments of Kilmartin Glen, Poltalloch has produced evidence of many burials in cists, some with decorated slabs in them. Although less compelling or visually exciting than the sites on the glen floor, lying as it does in a rather untidy disturbed landscape, this old gravel quarry is very important to an understanding of prehistory.

North Poltalloch (NR 823 976-820 971)

Here are two distinct archaeological sites: this and another south of Poltalloch House. The locations of decorated cist slabs which now lie among the remains of gravel extraction have produced a strange setting. The gravel has been removed from around them, making them appear to lie on mounds instead of being just below ground level. In 1928-9 the site was recorded by J. H. Craw, but before him there had been reports of disturbed and robbed cists in the Poltalloch area. Allegedly this was the work of a factor called Gow, who opened a number of them and removed their contents. Once they were in the hands of his sister after his death the objects disappeared without being recorded.

One consuming interest of Mr Craw was the discovery of a beautiful jet necklace in one of three cists. He linked it to another found in the Kilmartin Glebe Cairn, sadly now lost without trace. He recorded the Old Poltalloch sites as being a continuation of the line of cairns that stretches from the north 4 1/2 miles in length parallel to the Kilmartin Burn. The cists were discovered in the gravel bank that flanks Kilmartin Glen to the west. The north of this raised beach is at a promontory at Slockavullin, where there is rock art on an outcrop. The south end of the deposit is on a similar promontory with a small stream curling round it. He says: 'The crest of the promontory has been used as a gravel pit for many years. It is known as *Brouch an Drummin* (the brae of the elder bushes), but the old name is *Kill y Kiaran* (the cell or the burying-ground of St. Kiaran). This fits with what was disturbed at the quarry, for there were two clusters of graves, one group prehistoric and one late medieval. The whole site had the remains of a low, curving mound to the north, and a standing stone.

The first cist had been found in 1910 on the slight mound that ended the promontory. A second cist, excavated in 1928 (with great difficulty because it had the roots of an ancient elm tree growing through it, and took 6 ½ hours to clear) was made of four slabs of schist, the end slabs lying inside the long ones, with a covering slab. He wrote: 'The contents of the cist were a jet necklace, a flint knife, fragments of possibly cremated human bones and teeth, a few pieces of charcoal and lumps of ochre.' Bones and charcoal were at opposite ends of the cist to the necklace and knife. Trenching of the rest of the knoll did not reveal any signs of a cairn above it, but the 'stone may have been removed when the ground was under cultivation' – another piece of useful information about the site. A third cist was covered with a capstone that was too long for it, and had sharp tool markings underneath to reduce its thickness. The floor of the cist was paved with 69 'small, flat, water-worn stones'. The cist slabs were grooved 'with a tool similar to that used on the cover'. Grooves were made to slot the end slabs into the side slabs similar to those on the plain below, and he concluded 'it is probable that they were made by the same people'. These grooves are a characteristic of this area, and are generally rare. The cist had bones, teeth, charcoal, ochre and a damaged and fragile early Bronze Age Food Vessel. The site of the standing stone was investigated with a trench 3.66m long that showed an undisturbed loam covered with a layer of small stones.

This was only the beginning, for gravel extraction did not stop. From 1960-62 four cists and two stone settings were exposed.

Settlement evidence is hard to find, but in 1959 a multi-period site had been found and was excavated between 1960-2. There were round and oval pits thought to be for cooking. One was backfilled then used as an oven, then replaced with two hearths surrounded by stone – an open-air cooking

92. Poltalloch jet necklace
(Crown Copyright RCAHMS)

place. It was noted that south of the low curved mound mentioned in 1928 there was a curving ditch, and parts of other ditches were found to the north. Within the ditched area there were around 60 post holes, some cut later than the 'cooking pits', and among these were the possible outlines of two circular timber buildings. Part of one floor was paved with rough slabs and there were packing stones in some large postholes. It was thought that the hearths belonged to this phase. The floor was covered with clay and another building constructed above it, made with an oak frame. This was destroyed by fire; grain and wattle and daub were found among the debris. To the west of the timber building were stone foundations, including a small round stone hut. Around it were signs of iron working. Glass beads dated this latest phase to 'the second half of the first millennium AD'. 'The site was called 'Bruach an Druimein''. At last there are some signs of where people lived, but efforts continue to discover more burial cists, for at the time of these discoveries four more cists and two stone settings came to light. One grave was destroyed by a mechanical digger, the scattered cist slabs including one with about 70 cups on its underside.

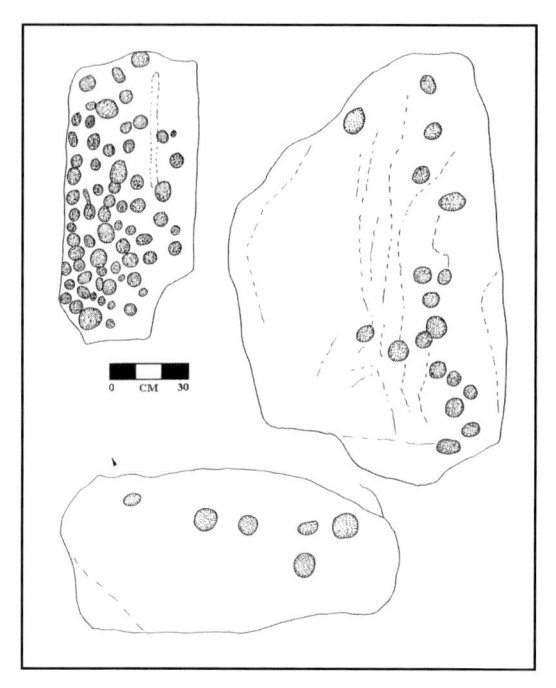

93. Three cup-marked slabs Poltalloch

A second cist had a floor of pebbles discoloured by burning. In it there was a beaker. Another cist contained a food vessel in a shallow pit.

A fourth cist had a floor made of rounded pebbles. The capstone had 12 plain cups on the underside and one end slab had a single cup on its inner face and several others on the back. Here a young adult had been buried with a Food Vessel and a plano-convex knife.

This is a very important key to understanding how rock art was used. Open-air rock art is designed to be seen prominently in the landscape, open to the skies. In cists, the art is buried, face down, establishing a special relationship with the people buried there. It was never intended to be seen by anyone else. The date of the burials coincides with the date of the pottery and other artefacts. Beakers, Food Vessels and plano-convex knives (flint knives that are made from a curved flake and worked on the top and along the sides, leaving the curved under-surface free of marks) all belong to the late Neolithic/early Bronze Age, roughly 4000 years ago. The cup markings are put on the insides of the slabs facing into the burial, which gives them a special significance. Even if the slabs were cut from outcrop already decorated, its meaning would have changed according to its new use. The other recorded feature was a cluster of 11 small slabs around a paved circular floor and the remains of a second setting of stones. The pottery from the cists went to Duntrune Castle and the knife to the Royal Museum of Scotland.

In 1960 another cist was disturbed by a bulldozer. It contained a single burial but no grave goods. Another reported in 1961 was destroyed without any recorded details. The site today is very confusing. A halt has been called to further mechanical excavation, where there is little left to see. The cup-marked slabs are still there and appear to be lodged in mounds, artificially created by the removal of gravel from around them.

In front of cottages nearby is an outcrop rock that has cups and cup and ring marks. These are difficult to see because of what grows on them, but have been recorded by others (Naddair). Higher up the slopes that command a view of the main glen, in a fringe area that has extensive all-round views is Ballygowan.

Ballygowan (NR 816 977)

The site at Ballygowan (Tyness Cottage), now protected by railings and open to the public, is one of the earliest to be recorded. It first appeared in Simpson in 1864 and has featured in all literature since. The surface of the outcrop is as smooth as a gritty metamorphic rock will allow.

94. View from Ballygowan

The exposed outcrop has its motifs concentrated in the centre of the rock where they are framed like a picture. Whether this is because the rock was originally partly covered over when the markings were made or whether the decision to leave spaces around them was taken at the time is not known.

95. Ballygowan

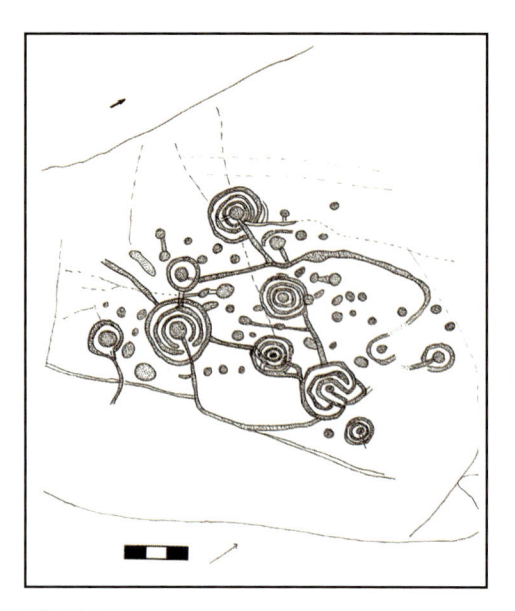

96. Ballygowan

The cups and rings concentrated in the central area are arranged on the downward slope to the east; some make use of natural cracks and scorings where ducts run from central cups or when motifs are linked by grooves. The motif at the highest NW point is a cup and three penannulars: two ducts lead from the cup, one in the direction of the most easterly large motif at the bottom, and the other to the side. Either by chance or by design an oval-shaped grooved enclosure is formed below with a cup and three rings at its centre, the rest being filled with cups of different shapes and sizes. The cup and rings have a groove from the outer ring leading down to the outer ring of an unusual motif at the bottom. This is a cup at the centre of an arc and two penannulars, the ends of which are joined; and from the cup the duct turns sharply to join an extension of the inner arc. Further below is a large cup with a duct and two concentric pear-shaped rings and a large linked satellite cup.

The oval enclosure is formed on the north by a groove that begins at the centre of the NW top motif, forms an arc round a cup and duct, swings out to the north, then bends towards the bottom large motif. The southern part of the oval is formed by a groove that begins at the same source. It is divided to the south where it joins a cup at the centre of two concentric rings. Below that is a large cup at the centre of three concentric rings which have a curved groove leading into the outer ring from the next cup, and duct that runs down the rock from the cup to end at a crack. Other motifs on either side of this oval formation are three large cups to the south, one with a duct and ring, and to the north are cups and a cup and penannular, with a groove curving from the cup towards the oval. What appears to be a rather random scatter of symbols does therefore have a number of focal points and a strong link between them. A low ridge with three cups is located 2.8m to the south. In a nearby enclosed field is a cup marked boulder.

The area in which these decorated rocks appear stands well above the monuments in the glen to the NE and east, with extensive views all around. To the west the land rises, undulates, with streams and irregular

97. Ballygowan

patches, towards Loch Michean, where there is another major panel marking the descent from the western high ground to the intermediate level of Ballygowan, before the descent to the glen. It is not clear whether this area was growing crops in prehistoric times (something that we would all like to know), but it certainly would have been good for pasture and hunting. The presence of marked rocks here is a link between streams and paths from the western high ground.

South Poltalloch (NR 812 963)

The ruins of Poltalloch House overlook pasture that slopes south towards the Crinan estuary via the Moine Mhor. By the time a fence crossing the pasture from east to west is reached, the land has become boggy where a spring rises, and the bent and other signs of marsh thicken further south. This may have been a place where water came up almost to the Mansion House. On either side of this low-lying land is outcrop rock. That to the west dips eastward, is covered with cracks, and has some outstanding rock art. On the opposite side of the shallow glen there are markings on outcrops. 100m NW of the walled garden other rock art is now inaccessible because it is so densely overgrown, and some of it was blown up in the nineteenth century to make a path.

98. Poltalloch location

99. Poltalloch west outcrop

The Western rock (NR 812 963)

The outcrop surface has natural cracks running from east to west and others from north to south. Some of the motifs have been split away where some of these cracks meet; in other parts of Britain such broken off slabs have been used for cist covers, and that is a distinct possibility here. Two panels are separated by grass, and to the south the centre of the panel is dominated by a cup at the centre of four widely-spaced and ungapped rings. Two cups are included in the outer ring, and five within the spaces between rings, perhaps already there before the newer, large motif was made. There are some scattered cups, and some are grouped. Others are central to concentric rings and have grooves running from them down the rock. The number of rings varies from one to five. Most occupy the west upper slope, where two of the cups are the centres of many-radiating grooves – an unusual feature.

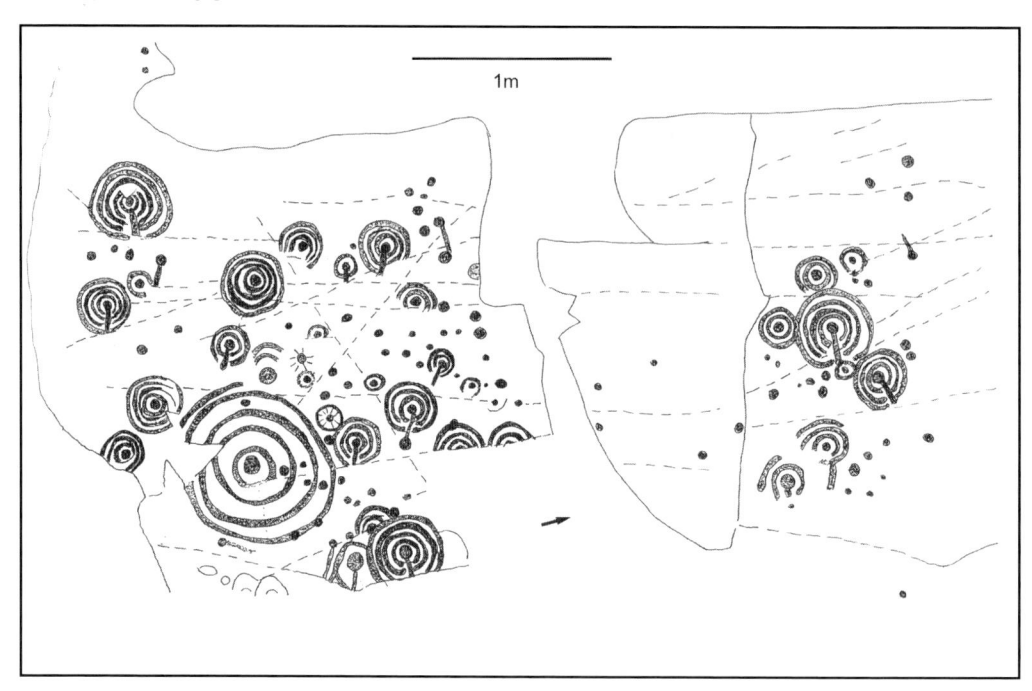

100. Poltalloch western rock

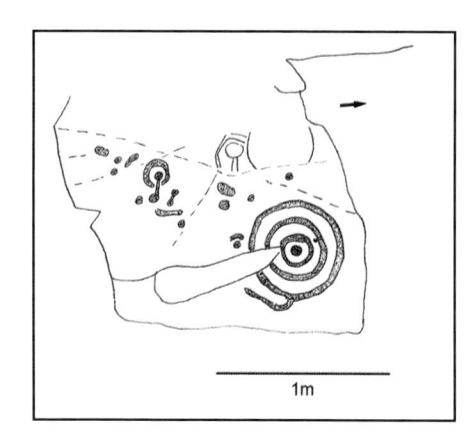

101. Poltalloch western rock

Ducts from cups end at cracks, or in one case in another cup. A crack that runs through the large central figure cuts two cup and ringed figures in half; part of the rock here must have been taken away after the motifs were made. The lower, east, slope has another figure of three well-spaced ungapped rings centred on a cup, with an extra groove attached to the outer ring. Part of it is damaged. Above it, west, are a cup, a duct and four rings that end at a crack that may have opened up naturally to remove the lower part of the figure. It is strongly made and has two attached motifs: a cup and two semi-circles and a cup, duct and angular ring – making it the dominant motif. Between the two major figures is an area enclosed by cracks that contains cups, cup and arc and single ring and grooves made by linking small cups.

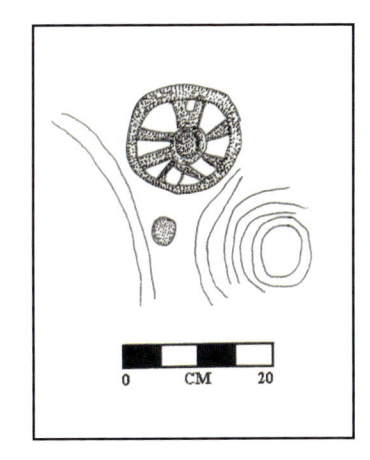

102. Detail of radiating grooves from a central cup

103. Radiating grooves

The north part has a focus on a cup and duct with four penannulars, and rather angular concentric rings which ignore the cracks. A possibly later cup and two rings cut the outer ring to the south, and a circular motif touches the outer ring to the west where there are some scattered cups and a cup and arc. Below, the duct from the central cup of the main motif reaches a cup and ring that touches a cup, duct, and three penannulars. Six cups are prominent in this section bounded by cracks, and some fainter ones. The bottom section has six cups, a cup at the centre of a penannular and arc and a cup at the centre of two linked grooves, and an outer arc. The southern extension of this outcrop has two small cups and rings and three small cups. The depth of some of the motifs is an outstanding characteristic, and so are the spaced, ungapped rings of two of the larger motifs (to be compared with Achnabreck). The sculptors have used the natural zoning caused by cracks to arrange groups of motifs. The 'star pattern' radiates are rare; there is a mixture of gapped and ungapped rings and some penannulars. Many of the cups may have been on the rock before other motifs were added.

Site 2. (NR 815 968)

There is another group of motifs 100m north west of the walled garden, but the dense vegetation cover and restrictions imposed by the danger of a large crumbling building have made it impossible to view it. A 1933 photograph shows a multi-ringed motif similar to that on the western rock. Apparently many other motifs were destroyed in the nineteenth century when part of the outcrop was blown up to make way for a path.

Site 3 (NR 815 962)

East of Site 1 is another prominent outcrop with the road to the church running past its eastern edge, giving extensive views in all directions. Motifs have been discovered here recently (Naddair). As these were re-covered after the excavation, only a glimpse is available.

104. Poltalloch east.

These sites flank what is an important shallow glen that runs towards the sea, and it is possible that these sites rose above an inlet. They form a part of a larger group that follows a distinct line, including cairns and other ritual monuments. There is a cist and standing stone south of Rowantree Lodge, three cists south of Barsloisnoch Lodge, and close to the Crinan estuary are the remains of a cairn and a standing stone. This forms a 'ritual' corridor from the sea into Kilmartin Glen. One of the Barsloisnoch cists (NR 813 956) has a groove to hold the end slab; the west side slab has three grooves, and the inner side slab has two adjacent cupmarks. This and the other cist were excavated by Craw in 1929. Low mounds surrounding the cists may have been created during field clearance.

MONUMENTS

The Old Poltalloch area, the Carn Ban cairn and the Badden slab have already given an indication of the use of cup marks on the underside of cist slabs and of the incorporation of pecked linear designs into cists. The outstanding monuments of Kilmartin Glen are here examined. The trouble with large, exposed cairns is that they attract treasure-seekers and clumsy digs that are more likely to cause damage and destruction than yield discovery and record. Visitors today have access to many sites in controlled conditions. Exploring these sites, the main emphasis has been on those that incorporate rock art.

The Glebe Cairn (NR 833 989)

At the north of the glen close to the village of Kilmartin itself, the Glebe cairn that is so clearly visible from the village has no reported rock art, but it is part of the line of cairns that is such an important and prominent feature of the landscape. Its shape today is misleading. It was over 30m diameter and 4m high before reconstruction. In 1864 Canon Greenwell (of Durham: excavator of barrows and cairns all over Britain) found two concentric rings of boulders in the SW quadrant. A cist at the centre of one circular setting was made of four side slabs and a cover. Inside was a Food Vessel and a jet necklace, dating it to the late Neolithic/early Bronze Age, around 4000 years ago. No trace remained of human remains. There was a cist at the centre of the cairn and a hollow sunk into the gravel covered with a large slab of schist. Fragments of a Food Vessel were found in it, 'a quantity of black unctuous matter', and the rest was filled with gravel.

Nether Largie North cairn (NR 830 984)

105. Nether Largie North end cist slab (R. Morris)

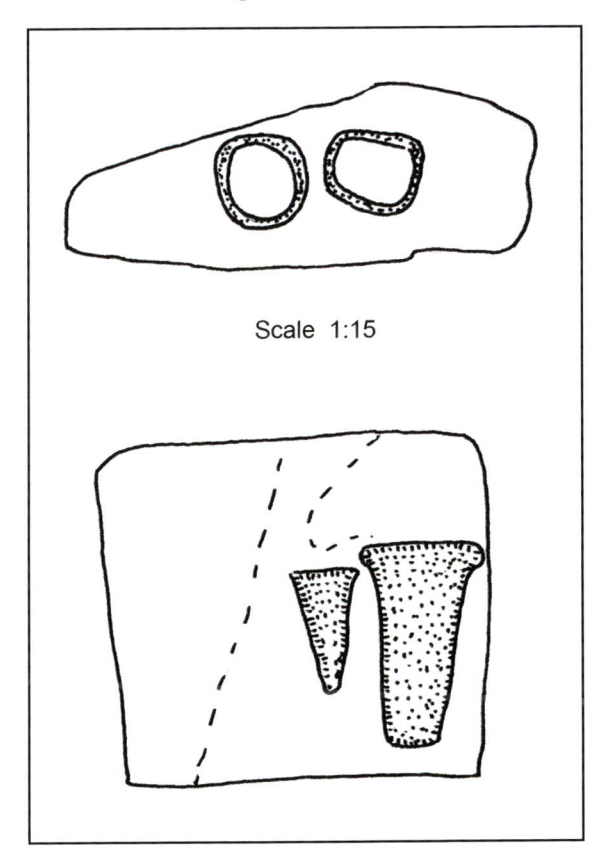

Scale 1:15

106. Nether Largie North cairn: upright slab possibly from another cist, and the end slab of the existing cist.

This cairn was completely excavated in 1930. After that it was reinstated 21.6m and 20m in diameter. Without kerbs, it was 2.7m high. The excavator, Mr. Craw, said that the central area was enclosed in a bank of stones. Roughly at the centre was a massive cist set into a pit dug into the gravel. It had about 40 cups and at least 10 axeheads on the underside of the capstone, and 18 flat slabs lay on top of the cist cover. The cist contained soil with a human molar, some ochre and some charcoal fragments.

The inner face of the north end slab had two axe carvings on the inside.

To the south of this cist was an arrangement of slabs that might have been for another burial, although nothing was found. There were two upright slabs, the one at the east being decorated with two pecked circles. Although the whereabouts of the original are unknown, a cast of it is now in The Royal Museum, Edinburgh. 3.3m NE of the central pit was an oval pit dug into gravel, containing an ox tooth and charcoal fragments.

These finds seem surprisingly meagre for such a large burial operation. Only the cists, motifs and huge pile of stones testify to the importance of the site and ceremony.

The motifs

The rectangular block that was used as a cist cover with the motifs facing down into the grave has a natural split in one corner that creates a natural triangle marked with a cup; this suggests that when the cup was put on the rock it was already like that. There are cups and axe motifs, the axes apparently added later as some are superimposed on the cups. The cups vary in size and depth and appear to be randomly placed. Eight of the axes are complete, but they are shaped differently; most have an expanded cutting edge that identifies them as representations of metal axes. The butt ends are rounded. One is faintly pecked, perhaps a tentative beginning. Two are fragmentary, with no signs of any part of them being removed. Six of the axes incorporate cups. There is nothing straightforward about this arrangement of cups and axes; the symbols could belong to two periods of prehistory, although there is no reason to suppose that cup marks were no longer made at a time when metal was introduced.

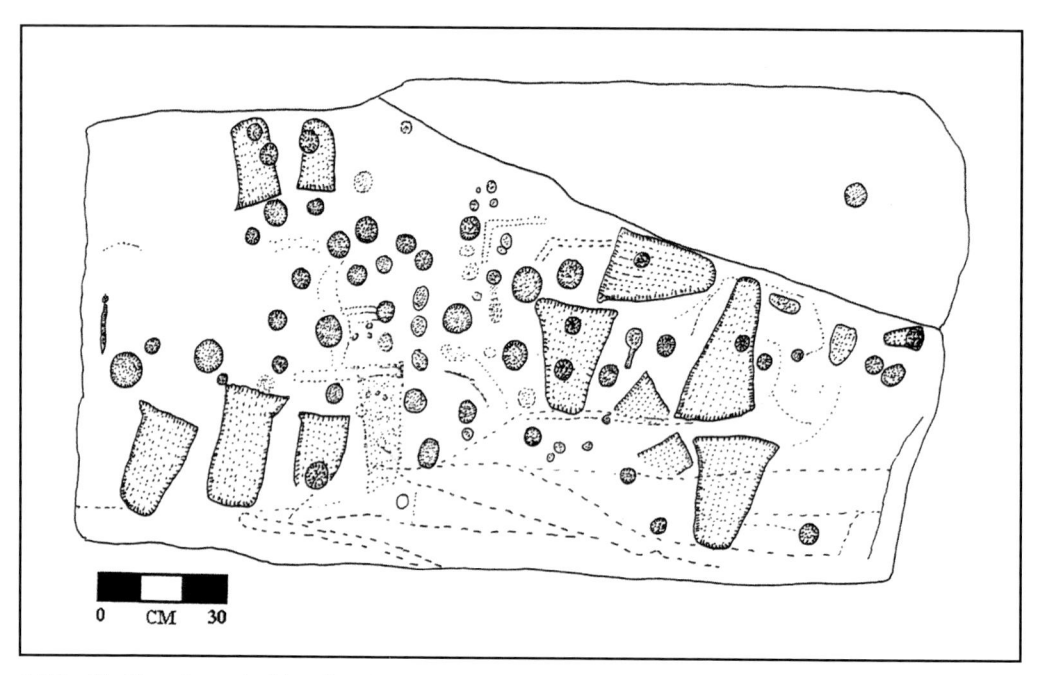

107. Nether Largie North cist slab.

There is some speculation that the slab was once a standing stone, reused. It could have been a piece of decorated outcrop cut off for use in a cist (there are other examples in Britain). In a non-metal age, cup marks were made with a sharp pointed stone tool, the impact clear in many examples. The axes seem to have been picked out with something fine and sharp, but that too could have been stone, as copper or bronze would be blunted against a harder surface. Whatever tool was used, the axes show the last period in which the cist cover was decorated, and the form of these axes gives the date of the burial as an early metal age. There is always an overlap in technology, so for a time stone tools and metal tools would have been in use together.

74

Nobody shouted "All change" at the end of the Stone Age so that the Bronze Age could begin! The symbols were not meant to be seen, and became a private matter between the dead and the living who buried them. That they are buried symbols gives them a different meaning and use from those in the open air. In the same cist the end slab had a large and a small axe, with the decorated surface facing into the grave. The larger of the axes has a flat butt end and a distinctive expanding blade that makes use of a fault in the fairly smooth rock surface to form the blade edge. The smaller axe stands lengthways and parallel beside it, its shape being more triangular. The two axes are framed by the edges of the slab and by an oblique fault to the left (see illustration nos. 105, 106).

Decorated outcrop (NR 830 984)

Not easy to see today is the decorated outcrop that slopes towards the cairn from the west next to the public path that is part of an ancient route. Some of these cup marks and an oval cup peep through the thin grass. Here is a link between simple art in the landscape and its use in burials. I have not been able to draw this outcrop, as it has had to remain covered. It is likely that there is more decoration along this ridge; I suspect what we can see represents a fraction of what exists.

Nether Largie Mid cairn (NR 830 983)

The cairn, excavated in 1929, is built on a low terrace. It was about 30m in diameter and 3m high when it was first recorded. Much of the cairn material was removed in the 1920s to repair roads - something that has happened in other parts of Britain. Two cists were excavated. The more northerly was set in a pit (now marked by concrete posts) and paved with flat slabs. The side slabs had been grooved to take the end slabs. The cist was empty. The south cist was inserted into a pit cut into the gravel and can be seen today with its huge capstone propped up with metal. This too was empty. A cup mark is reported on the NW end slab and at the centre of the slab is 'a pecked marking of a bronze axehead' 150mm long, 110mm broad at the blade and 70mm broad at the butt. The empty cists were not thought to have been disturbed.

9.5m NE of the south cist 'there is a slab measuring 0.95m by 0.63m and 0.21m in thickness, bearing 5 cupmarks up to 50mm in diameter and 10mm in depth'. It is difficult to reconcile what is visible today with some of the reports, especially Childe's reported 'grooved side slabs with cup and ring marks.'

108. Mid Nether Largie cairn

Nether Largie South chambered cairn (NR 828 979)

109. Nether Largie South, Clyde type cairn, looking towards Kilmartin.

Although there are no reported cup marks in this cairn, it is noteworthy as one of the oldest structures in Kilmartin Glen. (See also illustration no.8)

The roofing slabs and back slab, seen from the SSW show that it is constructed as a chambered cairn. Inside, this chamber is fully visible as of the Clyde type, a series of compartments of upright slabs and septal slabs, with gaps filled in with a drystone walling technique. In the rear compartment Greenwell found fragments of a Beaker and burnt bone in a small cist. There was a cremation north of this, and further north still the cremations became thicker, containing three broken and two perfect equal barbed and tanged arrows, flint flakes, broken quartz pebbles and an ox tooth. More Beaker fragments appeared in the continuing black layer on the floor of the chamber, and a round-based Neolithic vessel came from the north part of the cist. The third chamber held dark matter, cremated bones and an early undecorated pot mixed up with Beaker sherds. The outer chamber had unburned bone and pottery in the upper layers and some flint.

Two other cists were found under the cairn. One is now buried, but the other is a massive construction at the SSW, still visible, and empty when it was dug out. Although the Beaker and arrowheads belong to the late Neolithic/early Bronze Age, other pottery and the construction of the cairn point to its being built earlier than the others in the glen, and used over a long period of time. In a sense, it shares this long use with the Temple Wood circles.

Ri Cruin (NR 825 971)

Excavations in 1870, 1929 and 1936 at Ri Cruin revealed the complex history of this cairn. What we see today is largely a reconstruction, and the exposure of cists is something that would not have been seen in prehistoric times.

The most northerly visible cist was set in a central pit covered with a massive slab. The floor was covered with a slab and packed around with small boulders. The side slabs had grooves to fit the north end slab. Before the first excavation the grave had probably been robbed, so there is no record of what was in it. 7m to the SSE inside the kerb are the side slabs of a second cist, now collapsed. They are grooved at the west end to fit in the end slabs. Nothing was found in it. The third cist lies outside the kerb edge, set in a pit, made of upright slabs, and two paired slabs at each side. The west end slab has seven pecked axes. At the east end a narrow vertical slab with unusual decoration was found, but this was destroyed in a fire at Poltalloch House. A cast is preserved at the Royal Museum, Edinburgh.

110. Ri Cruin cairn

111. Ri Cruin cairn cist with axes on the inner end slab.

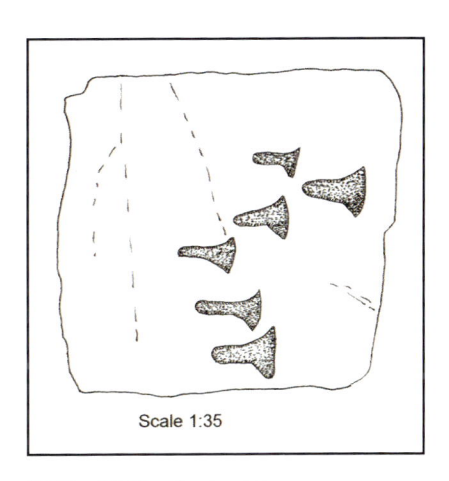

112. Ri Cruin axes.

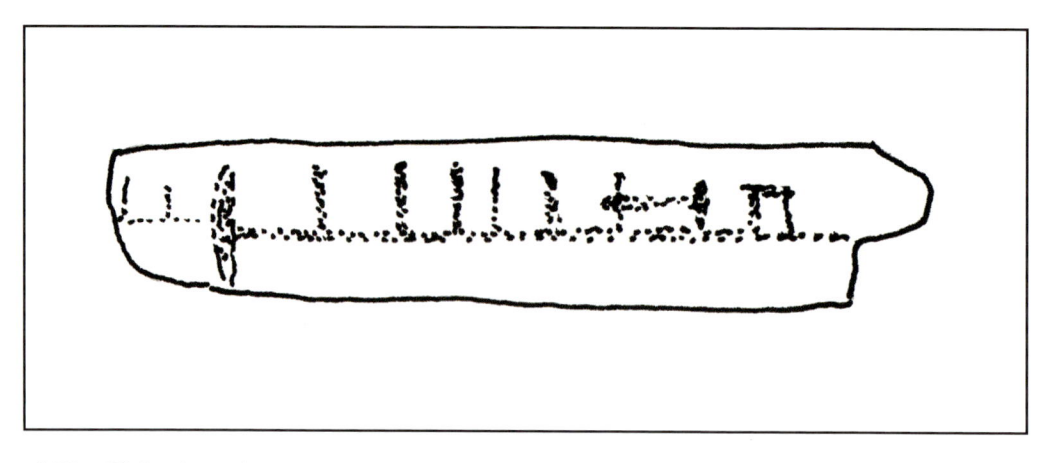

113. Ri Cruin cairn vertical stone with linear design (c. 1m long)

The decoration is a vertical line from which small lines branch out at right angles. Four of these lines are linked to form two boxes. No one knows what this represents, but this does not preclude speculation.

The site was used for lime burning in more recent times.

Baluachraig (NR 831 969)

The three divisions of this sloping rock outcrop give an extensive view in all directions over Kilmartin Glen, but high ground cuts out any further view to the east. It lies slightly above the present valley floor, not at a particularly high point.

114. Baluachraig location.

The outstanding features of the decoration on the south part of the main outcrop are three rows of cups, some with single rings, arranged into a triangular pattern. They follow the direction of a natural crack. Another crack meets this obliquely, forming a triangular enclosed surface, the shape of which is followed by the arrangement of cups and cups with rings.

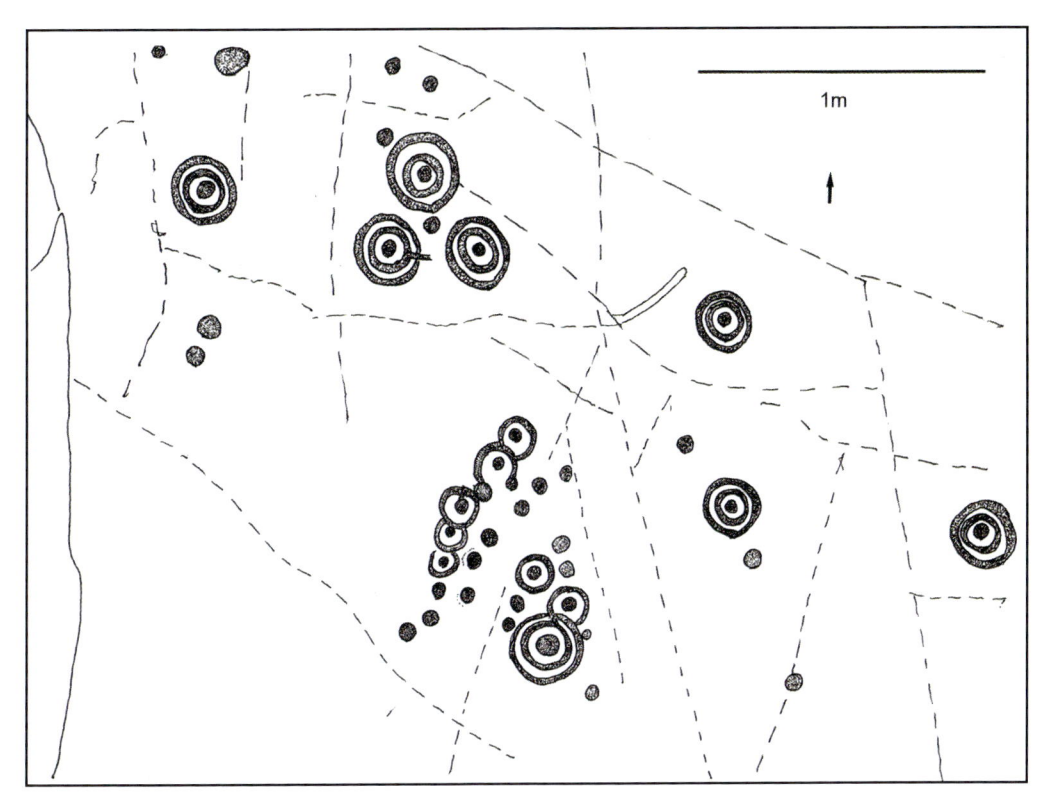

115. Detail of Baluachraig, south.

116. Baluachraig, south detail.

A crack that runs from east to west encloses other motifs to the south: cups and two cups with two rings each. On the whole rock the motifs are mainly cups and cups with no more than two ungapped rings. This gives the impression that they were made there by the same people at the same time. Most of the ringed motifs are clustered towards the crack at the southern end, and the divisions formed by cracks seem to influence the position of others. As the surface narrows to a north-pointing promontory, one section has cups almost exclusively, and the end has cups and rings. An interesting observation was made in 2003 that the western edge of this rock has a series of close parallel grooves that may have been mistaken as plough or harrow lines, but they are restricted to one area and too close for that. When they were made and what they represent is not known. To the north is another piece of outcrop with a cup and a cup and ring.

117. Baluachraig detail - parallel lines, are they ancient or modern?

To the west another part of the outcrop has ten cups. Today the site is fenced by iron railings, with access by stile. It lies north of a concentration of very interesting prehistoric monuments, some of which have cups and rings.

The nearest surviving monument is the **Dunchraigaig cairn** (NR 833 963) that lies on a terrace 230m SE of the site just described, at a higher level, separated from it by a small stream.

30m in diameter, it is a huge pile of water-worn boulders over 2m high. At first a slot in the south side, like a stone letterbox, is puzzling. Excavations that have taken place since 1864 have established that there was a cist in the middle, made of slabs and containing an extended burial accompanied by a Food Vessel with cremated bone, charcoal, flint flakes, sand, gravel and clay. Under a floor of paving was a crouched burial. A second cist, now covered over, was partly filled with gravel, on the surface of which was a Food Vessel, cremated bone and flint flakes. A third cist, thought by Canon Greenwell to be the primary one, lies SE of the centre, its pit dug into the old ground surface and its sides made like a drystone wall. Over it was a massive capstone, and the cist contained burnt and unburned bones of eight to ten people buried with a whetstone, a greenstone axe, flint knife and pottery fragments.

118. Dunchraigaig cairn.

Ballymeanoch henge, kerbed cairn, cairn and standing stones

The next group of monuments forms an unusual concentration, giving the whole area a very important ritual significance, open in all directions, and apparently focused on high ground to the east.

The Henge (NR 833 692)

119. A henge, foreground, with the remains of an excavated cist (right).

Henges are rare. This one is made up of a ditch with an external earth and stone wall, excavated from the ditch, with an entrance causeway running right through it. It is 40m in diameter. In 1864 Canon Greenwell discovered in his excavation two cists that can still be seen. The larger is central, with long side slabs, a floor of rounded pebbles and a massive cover. He found nothing in it, for it had been dug into before.

The second cist, to the NE, had four slabs and a cover, containing three inhumations and a Beaker. It is likely that they belong to the same period as the henge itself. A report in DES of 1995 tells of the discovery of two faint cup marks on a flat stone that may be the missing north slab of this cist in the centre of the henge. It was left in situ in the ditch.

The Cairns (NR 835 963 and 833 964)

Nearby are two cairns. One, covered with turf, is 30m in diameter and over 1m high. It is made of boulders covered with earth. Craw's excavation of 1928 encountered charcoal at ground level but no signs of burial. About 30m NW of the standing stones is a kerbed cairn 7m in diameter and 0.7m high. The kerbs are boulders, some of which have been robbed out, and may have been graded in height.

Standing stones (NR 933 964)

The standing stones are very impressive and create a special atmosphere with their stillness, arrangement, size and setting. Of particular interest are three with motifs.

Out of seven standing there are settings of two and four in parallel lines. One fell down over 100 years ago, the stump was excavated and its remains were dumped close to the kerbed cairn just described above.

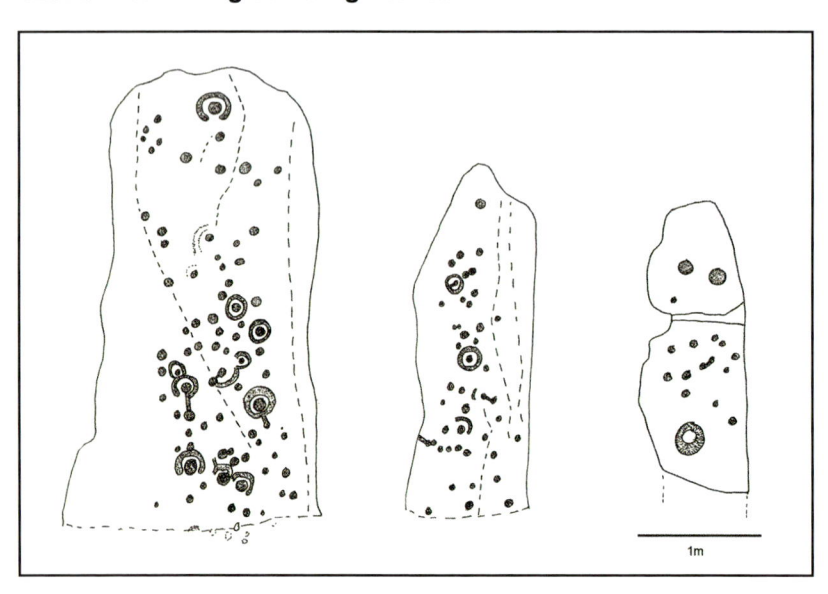

120. Six surviving standing stones

121. Drawings of two decorated standing stones and a fallen standing stone, part of which remains on site.

The line of four stones has the tallest to the north. The next south is extensively decorated on its flat, rectangular east face. The motifs seem to follow the line of an oblique crack. They are mostly well-finished cups; some have partial rings or arcs and three have ducts running from the ringed cups into a single cup. Some of the cups are known to lie below the present field level.

The next stone south is also decorated, this time on the west face, with mostly cups, some linked by a groove. At the pointed top of the stone is a cup with a faint ring. There is a prominent cup at centre of an ungapped ring in the middle of the stone, and two touching cups at the centre of a ring between the two. Many of the cups cluster together, and are linked to one another.

122. An impressive line

The third standing stone with markings, now lying half buried by the kerbed cairn, stood 18m WNW of the more northerly of the pair of stones that lie roughly parallel to the four. It is curiously decorated, the most prominent feature being an hourglass perforation that runs right through the stone face. Above that are small cups, two joined by a groove, but the top part has two large cups that look like eyes. No doubt this is how they would have appeared to people visiting the site in the past. But what of the hole? Did people have to look through it? At what? The stone stood in a pit that had three small patches of cremated bone in it. Was this some sort of foundation deposit? Was it human bone?

These seven stones make up part of a large complex of standing stones in Kilmartin Glen. What was the significance of their alignments? Had it anything to do with astronomy? Were they used in some dance-like ceremony? Were they pointing people in the direction of something important or away from something to be avoided? We will never know, but can speculate endlessly. Why not? They make good stories, and the stones and theories belong to all of us.

123. Part of the fallen standing stone

Temple Wood stone circles (NR 826 978)

It is difficult to reconcile W. Daniell's drawing of 1818 of a stone circle at Temple Wood with what we see today, but artists do select what is of most significance to them – in this case ten flat, similar slabs arranged around a pit, with a cairn in the background.

128. Temple Wood: an artist's view in 1818. W.Daniell

129. Temple Wood today.

The site was thoroughly excavated between 1974 and 1979 by J.G.Scott and reconstructed for display to the public. Before him the site had been dug superficially by J.H.Craw in 1929.

There are two circles at the site, close together. The earlier is the NE circle, seen as the flatter of the two. It began life as a circle of wooden posts (as many other British circles did) which were later replaced by stone ones. There are concrete markers that show two phases of activity. The stone circle might not have been completed, as the action moved to the more prominent of the two: a circle of 22 standing stones to the SW. We know from the carbon dates that the circle was dismantled in prehistoric times and covered with cobbles.

Both circles were obviously of great ceremonial importance, and were connected in some way to rituals at nearby cairns and standing stones for part of their lives, but there is not enough detailed evidence to make fine distinctions in time. The later circle was itself modified by the addition of horizontal slabs to fill the spaces between the upright stones. There are two cup marks on one of them. The 'closing' of the monument must have been of significance, for what was enclosed was a cemetery – not the original use of a stone circle, but a modification. The disappearance of some of the standing stones is probably recent, and one in situ still has the beginnings of a millstone carved into it, showing for what it was intended.

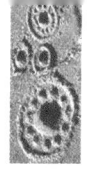

Two cists were constructed outside the circle on the NE and W, covered with cairns, constructed for inhumations The former was surrounded by small kerbstones, some of which had been moved in antiquity. The large cist contained a Beaker, three barbed and tanged arrowheads and a flint scraper.

130. Temple Wood cupped spacer stone recorded during excavation.

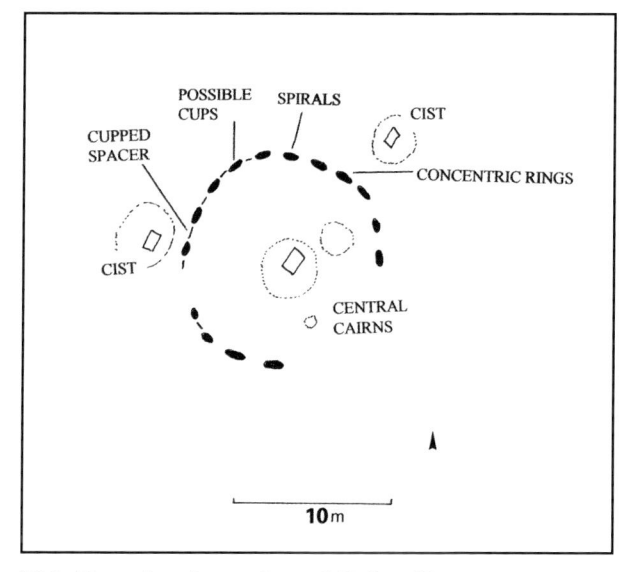

131. Drawing based on J.G.Scott.

The west cist had a flagstone floor, but only one tooth identified the burial of a child 4-6 years old. The large capstone was covered with a cairn, with a carefully constructed kerb of upright stones with dry-stone walling in between. There were other burials in the circle. At its centre was a large cist made of four slabs set in a pit half sunk below ground level. Its capstone had been removed before the early 19th century. Around the cairn that covered the cist was a kerb of upright slabs, many destroyed recently (so what we see today is largely a reconstruction). It contained cremations. To the NE a small kerbed cairn that covered a cist with a cremation, is covered with a big slab. SE of the central burial was a pit containing a cremation.

The two circles represent about 1000 years of history – about the same length of time as from the Norman Conquest to today. A few burials found within and around the second circle suggests a change of function from ceremonial to burial (on the other hand burial is itself ceremonial). The Beaker and flints make this a late event, for they belong to the late Neolithic/early Bronze Age. Although the 'closing' horizontal slabs probably belong to the period when the circle changed its function and have cup marks, the more prominent rock art is a linked spiral and two concentric rings. These could have been put on the standing stones at any time in history.

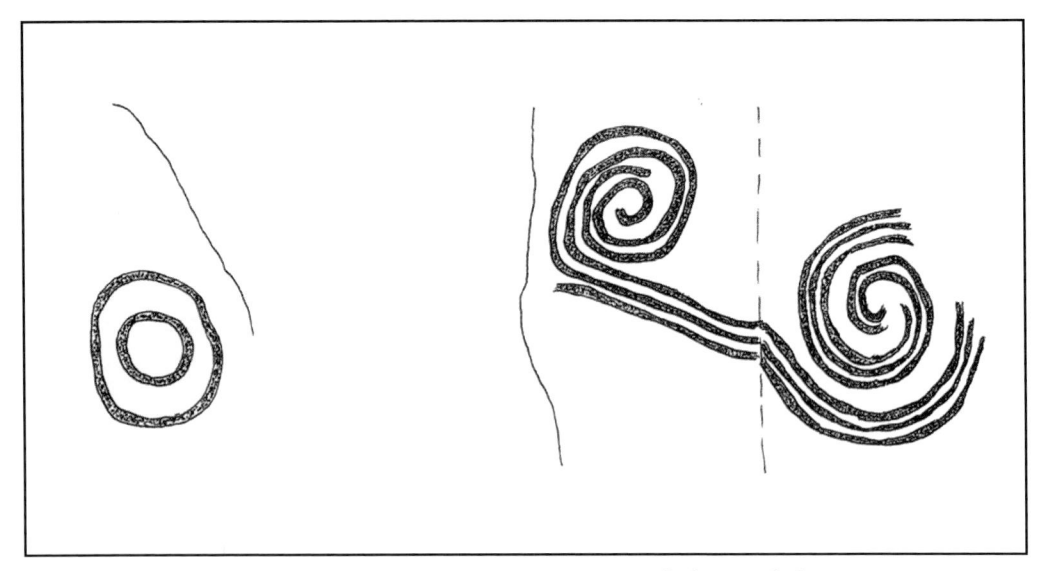

132. Double spirals and concentric rings on two of the uprights.

133. Concentric circles on an upright stone.

Spirals in rock art are rare, and the linked spiral is even rarer. Attempts to connect these with passage grave art in Ireland do not allow for the fact that they could have been invented here. The profuse and varied spirals on the Morwick cliff near Warkworth (Northumberland) are on the east coast: not exactly the best place to receive influences from across the Irish Sea! There are horned spirals at Achnabreck, but this type is unique. Perhaps it was created by someone with some originality. The concentric circles on the other stone are unlike others in the region in that they have no central cup, but that is not unique. No assumptions can be made about *when*

134. Detail of spirals (taken over 20 years ago)

these markings were put on, but we can say that the pecking of motifs gives these stones a special quality and place in the circle. Such is the limit of current knowledge. What is even more special about this design is that instead of having a single spiralling line, it starts with two parallel grooves that turn into three and then round a corner of the rock to decorate it on two faces.

Apart from its rock art, Temple Wood has a special place in the archaeology of the region, as it shows how much can be learned about a site by modern excavation. It also demonstrates that no matter how thoroughly this is carried out, it can never reveal the whole story of what happened there.

19th century print of standing stones at Ballymeanoch. Sir J.Simpson

89

8. The West

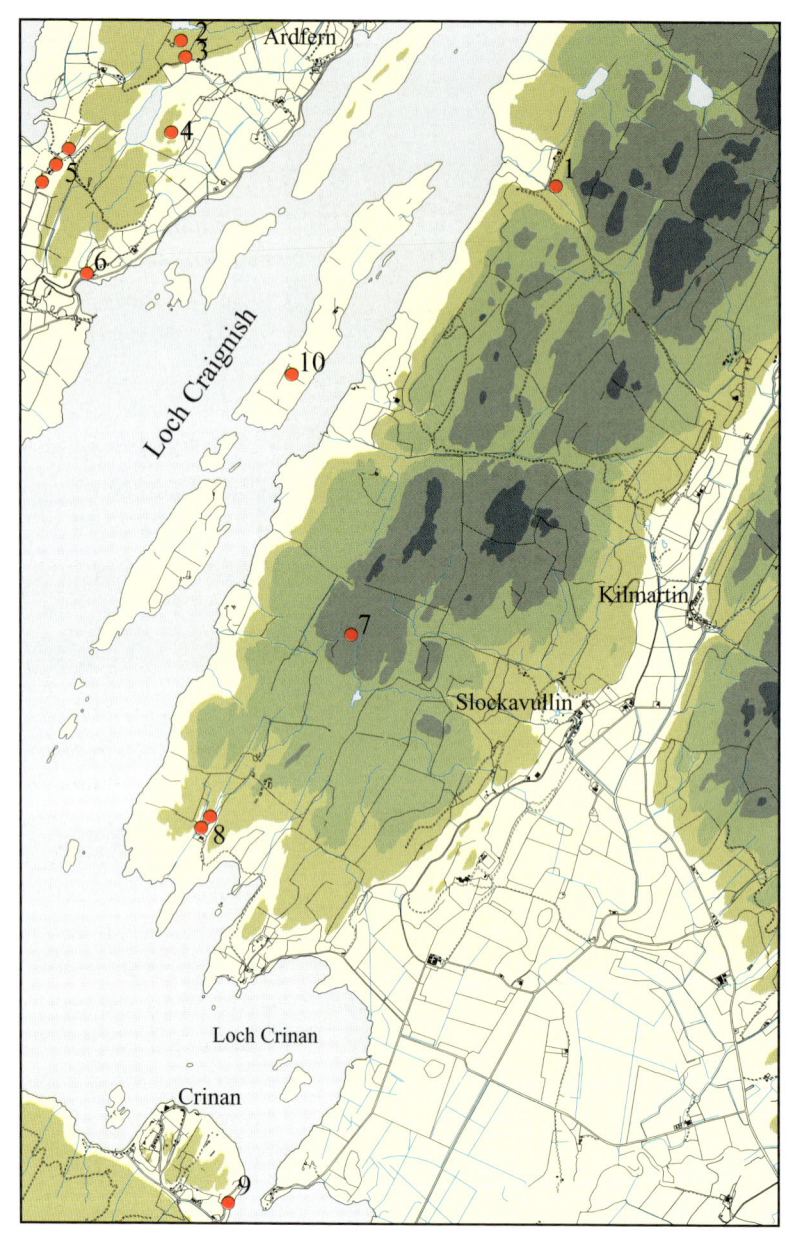

135. Site Location Map - The West

1. Ormaig
2 & 3. Barrackan
4. Duine
5. Achanarnich
6. Dun Mhuilig
7. Loch Michean
8. Ardifuir
9. Crinan Ferry
10. Dun Righ, Eilean Righ

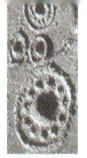

There are few places with such a beautiful coastline. The islands of Shuna, Luing, Lunga, Scarba and Jura, as well as some much smaller isles, stand off the coast to the west to offer some protection from Atlantic seas. The indented coast has a number of small inlets and bays navigable by small boats.

136. The west coast from the hinterland.

137. Kintraw: a prehistoric site that includes a cairn and large standing stone dominating the landscape.

The most northerly part of this survey is **Kintraw**, where the Barbreck River flows through Glen Domhain SW to reach Loch Craignish. Here, the low-lying land at the head of the loch is distinguished by a tall standing stone and cairn. 700m SSE of **Kilbride** (not to be confused with the Kilbride in Chapter 10) at NM 838 077 is a sand and gravel quarry area where several cists have been found during extraction, the earliest finds being reported in 1915. The glen is marked with standing stones and cairns. During the RCAHMS survey of 1982 a ruined cist was found containing the remains of an adult male and a flint knife. The inside of the ENE side slab 'appears to have been decorated with three roughly pecked motifs, probably axes'. The flint and the stone were reported to be 'preserved at Craigdhu' where the river enters the loch (RCAHMS 1988. No.98, page 99). Follow the coast south westwards and one emerges at Ormaig, high above the loch and its elongated small islands.

Ormaig (NM 822 027)

The marked outcrops are some of the most extensive and important in Britain, yet are badly managed, as planted trees obscure them and the route to them is not sign-posted. Here the crowding of rock surfaces with motifs, the use of the distinctive 'rosette' design and the fantastic views from the top of the hill to the loch and beyond combine to create a breathtaking experience.

138. The site of Ormaig in a forest clearing on the left.

It is possible to reach the site from Carnassarie Castle through pasture and planted forest via a path that roughly follows a wall and the forest edge as you near the site. As the loch is sighted, the path dips to the loch at a place where trees have recently been felled. There is a small stream to the right that forms a minor glen. Once this is crossed there is an indeterminate path along the side of the Creag Mhor hill through the trees that bends to the left, leading to an open space where the first decorated outcrops appear. The rest are under coniferous forest that grows thicker and more uncomfortable each year, making it difficult to see any of the other rock art. Fortunately the motifs were recorded before this situation developed. It is difficult to determine which viewpoints are covered from here because of the trees, but the site is a dominant viewpoint towards the loch.

139. The loch below Ormaig, with sheltered access to the sea.

Description

The rounded, ice-smoothed outcrops that are positioned over a glen that leads to the loch inlet has many different kinds of motifs, including rosette designs that are unique in Argyll but not in Northumberland (where they occur at three separate sites) and elsewhere. The lower sheet of rock has been exposed for some time, as two Campbell names dated 1874 and 1877 carved on the rock testify. This part of the rock has large and small cups with some grooves.

140. The western rock, which has additional names carved on it.

Further south the decoration is mainly of well-made large and small cups, some with rings, but the outstanding motif is the rosette made by arranging a circle of cups around a central cup, then encircling the whole thing in a ring. The largest and clearest is at the eastern edge. Beside it to the right (N) is a cluster of cups arranged in a roughly triangular form. The group is bounded on the west by a long narrow crack that also encloses five other ringed figures to the south, including two rosettes. There are two very large cups, the edges of which are truncated at a thin crack.

Above them (W) is another zone defined by cracks that contains a rosette, large and small cups, and 18 ringed cups. There are no ducts running from the cups. There is another triangle of cups and two parallel grooves. Above these are more large and small cups, four with arcs.

141. Ormaig rosettes in 2004.

142. Ormaig rosettes.

One particularly interesting feature here is the truncation of motifs by cracks – not that the cracks break through them, but they stop at the cracks. The second part of the outcrop, now in plantation, and very difficult to access, has some unusual closely packed motifs that make the site unique.

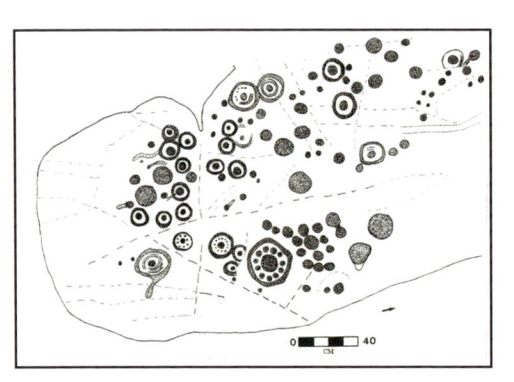

143. Eastern rosettes.

A long strip of rock has a part rosette at its west edge, perhaps incorporating two cups that were already there. In the same area are many clustered cups mostly free of arcs and rings. Further north, separated by a wide crack, the westerly slope has parallel grooves that ignore the natural cracks. Below them are two linked complex cup and ring motifs; the upper one has a central cup with another immediately below it, and five concentric rings. A duct from the cups and one from its outer ring are directed at the next motif; a cup and duct, two concentric rings and an outer third ring that opens out into a keyhole with the duct for the cup central. To the left of these two motifs are cups, some with ducts and some with arcs and single rings.

144. Ormaig: rock now almost covered with trees.

145. Ormaig north in the plantation.

146. The extreme north of the rock in the plantation.

147. The middle section of the rock in the plantation

148. Motifs at the south end of the rock

To the north the motifs jostle for space. A large cup is the centre of up to six concentric rings that seem to be superimposed on one another. There are many grooves running north to south, with a complex linking of cup and ring motifs in the same direction. At the north is a cluster of cups and single rings without ducts, as though calling a halt to this profusion of parallel lines.

There are other motifs on outcrops, but the forest has prevented us from examining them in any satisfactory detail. They are reported as having cups and cups and single rings, and numerous channels. It is a great pity that so much planting has obscured one of the most important sites in Scotland; maybe those responsible could be persuaded not to restock these hillsides so densely.

Barrackan

Barrackan is the name of a farm on the Loch Craignish peninsula, on the west side close to the sea. On high ground to the NE roughly between Lochs Fada and Mhic Mhairtein are two rock art sites. At NM 787 038, 21m north of the track to Barrackan is a boulder with 26 cups and one cup and ring. At NM 787 040, about 150m NNW of the above there are three groups of cups on a big rock sheet. One has 30 cups, another has three cups, a large cup and four small cups. The most northerly part has five cups and two connected cups (RCAHMS). Another marked rock is pictured in Morris (1977), but is not prehistoric. A reddish, smooth-topped schist boulder has two crosses divided by a mirror image of two Bs. Its position is NM 7794 0370, 175m WNW of the farm. The local name for it is 'The Priest Stone', and appears on the map as a 'cross incised stone'.

149. Barrackan

Duine (NM 786 032)

The site lies in planted forest south of the Barrackan sites and east of Loch Mhic Mhairtein. The farm after which it is named lies 700m to the SE. On a rock outcrop ridge on the SE side are 10 weathered cups and an oval (RCAHMS).

Achanarnich

The peninsula that encloses Loch Craignish to the SE has a cairn and chambered cairn at Ardfern. Although there are no reported prehistoric remains on the extreme tip of the peninsula, a walk to Craignish Point is full of interest and wild beauty. A small area of rig and furrowed land is witness to small-scale arable farming, now abandoned in favour of pasture. The entrance to Loch Crinan is part of the indented coast visible to the SE. The cup and ring marked rocks overlook the west coastline towards Scarba, Luing and Shuna. Other prehistoric features along this coast are duns and burial cairns. Craignish Castle lies SSW of the rock outcrops. Achanarnich is a farm house, and the main decorated outcrop lies 135m SW of it.

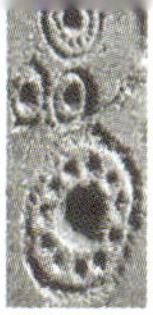

On a whaleback of outcrop (NM 774 027) that has become difficult to penetrate because of the growth of gorse there are patches of exposed rock that have motifs ranging from cups to a four-ringed motif at the centre of a cup. The ridge has extensive, beautiful views along the coast, and some earlier photographs give an uninterrupted view over bare rock. The most westerly patch of outcrop is split by cracks that run from N-S and some from E-W; in a panel framed by them is a cup at the centre of three ungapped rings with a fourth that stops at the crack. There is a small satellite cup. In the next panel to the north are cups in rows. One cup and five cups with a single ring are arranged in a domino formation, with another cup and ring in line. Two single ringed cups and other cups complete the section; to the north is a small detached piece of outcrop with a cup and two rings and a cup and three rings.

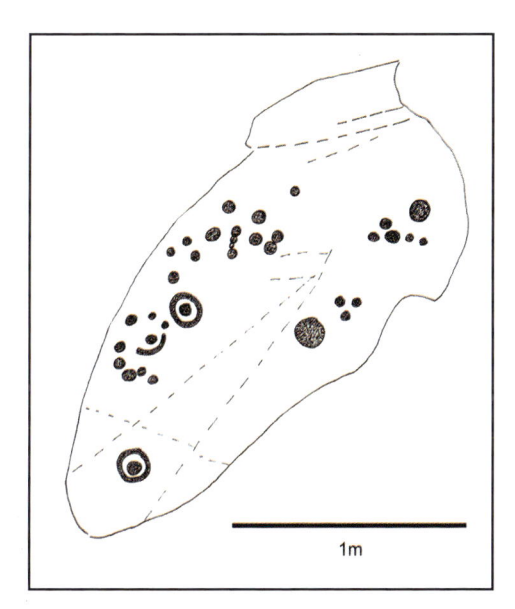

150. Achanarnich: cups with double rings.

152. South Achanarnich

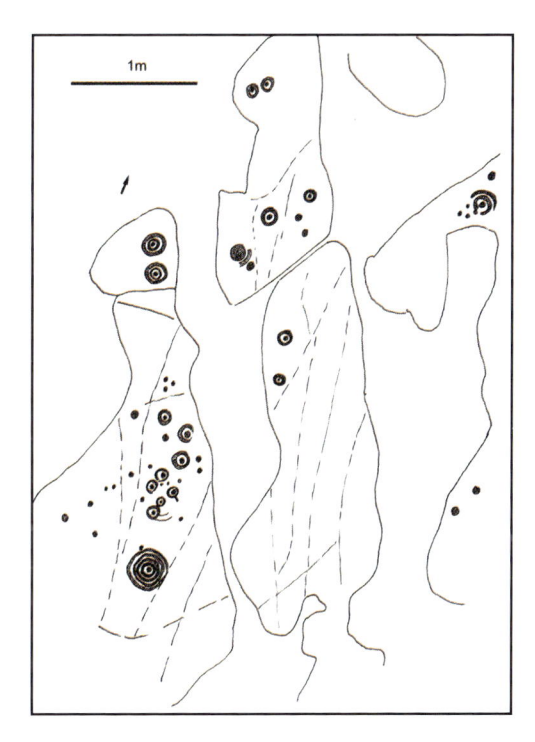

151. West Achanarnich

97

To the east is an elongated parallel sheet with multiple cups, large and small; two cups with single rings and a cup and arc clustered at the south end. The next section is clear apart from two cups with single rings to the north; finally to the north is a very large cup, four small cups and four cups with single rings.

Another parallel sheet to the east has two cups at its southern end, a cluster of cups at the north end and a cup, ring and arc. A rock sheet 60m north of Achanarnich (NM 775 028) has two groups of four and five cups.

SW of Cnoc Fraoich is a rock sheet with a cup and ring and 47 cups, most of them near the west edge of the sheet (NM 770 030).

Dun Mhuilig (NM 778 018)

Dun Mhuilig overlooks a small bay to the east into Loch Craignish. Just north of the Craignish to Ardfern road and 60m west of the Dun Mhuilig Cottages is a boulder with eight cups (RCAHMS).

Loch Michean (NR 803 987)

About 550m north of Loch Michean is a rock outcrop that emerges from the hillside at a place where a spring breaks out. The site is in a glen, yet a few metres higher is one of the most widespread and spectacular views of the west coast. Clearly the choice of this rock for marking is connected more with the spring than anything else.

153. Loch Michean, and the decorated rock inconspicuous at a spring.

The rock has not been illustrated before, and there is more on it than any previous description has given. Most of the motifs are clustered at the top half of the sloping outcrop. On the western edge are two basin-like cups and 19 others of different sizes in between the cracks that run down the slope. In this west section are four cups with single rings. One has a long duct connected to a cup; the other has a duct and is gapped. To the east is a cluster of ringed cups: six have single rings, one with a groove leading to a cup. There is a cup and gapped ring and a cup with two concentric rings. One large cup has a faint, broad ring. The lower part of the rock has ten cups and two cups with single rings.

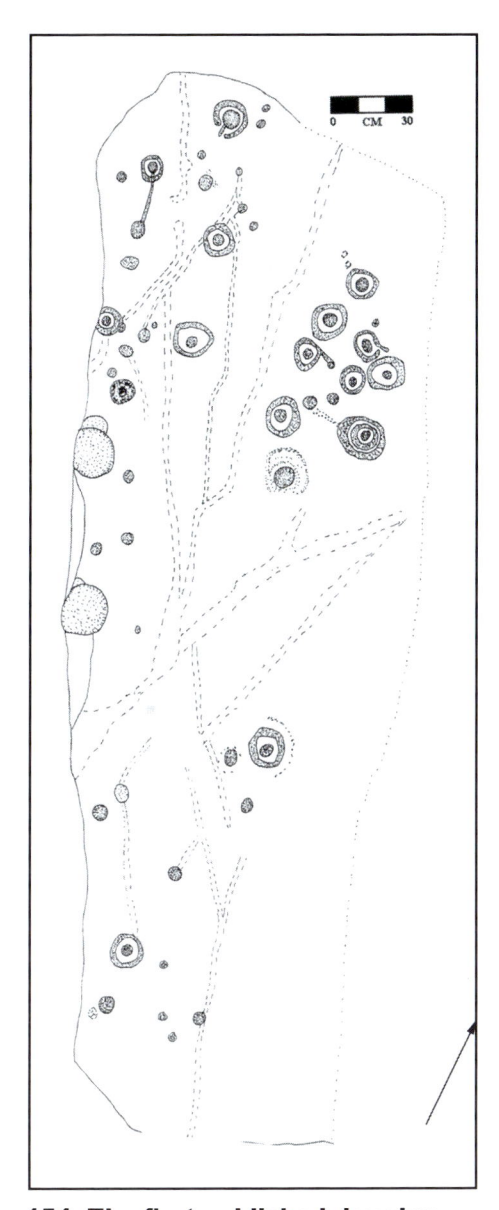

154. The first published drawing of Loch Michean motifs.

155. Large cups on the west edge.

156. The whole rock.

It has been said that the more complex the motifs, the higher up in the landscape they tend to be. This outcrop is much higher than most yet has only one motif with two rings, demonstrating the danger of generalisation. The importance of the site is that the trail leads from a spring source to the glen with a loch, then down to the Kilmartin plain. This is ideal stock-raising and hunting country, and is probably only one part of an above-coastal trail that runs from much further north. It continues south to Ardifuir, with the sea in sight.

Ardifuir

A glen that runs to the sea south of Ardifuir farmhouse has a central ridge of outcrop that leads down from higher ground and ends close to the sea with a distinctive group of paired cup marks. This ridge is the main focus of the rock art that follows it down at different levels. Some of the motifs are grassed over, but a few are visible. The glen continued to be of significance long after the motif makers used it, and there is an impressive dun next to the farmhouse. The glen, although open to the south, can have an enclosed feel to it, and attention is always directed to the sea. Today it provides sheltered pasture for sheep, and walls that cross the glen provide enclosures.

South

The most southerly panel came to light in 2003 with one or two cups showing in the grass. We recorded it and re-covered it.

157. The Ardifuir glen to the sea.

158. The most southerly of the Ardifuir motifs.

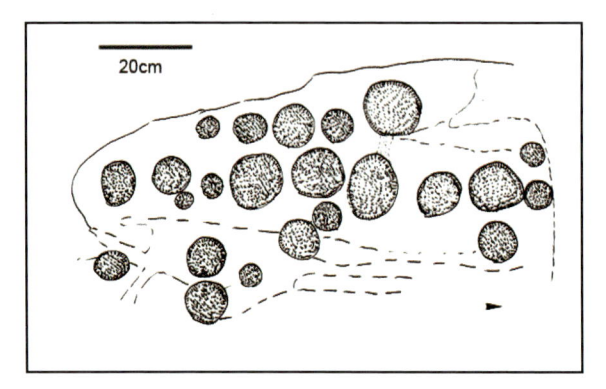

159. The most southerly rock.

North

The other sites are numbered according to an established system (RCAHMS). Most of them lie to the north of the farmhouse and the east-west enclosure wall.

1. North of the dun by the gate at the pasture walls is a boulder with two cups (NR 789 970).

2. 40m ESE of this is an outcrop with four cups on its east peak and three on its west (NR 789 969).

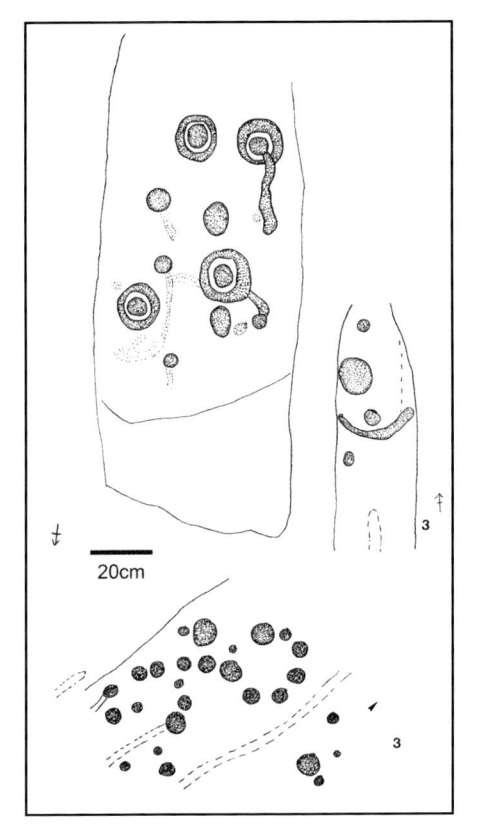

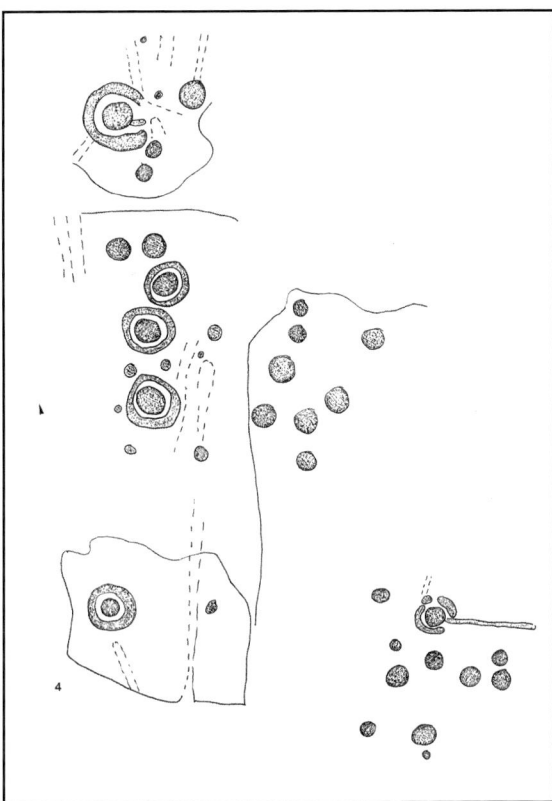

160. Ardifuir 3   **161. Ardifuir 4: a spread of cups and rings**

A wall that runs across the valley from east to west marks off the rest of the outcrops with motifs to the north. The outcrop is continuous, rising to the north, and shattered into smaller units, forming a tongue between two minor valleys. The marked rocks are so close together that they all share the same grid reference.

3. Just north of the wall and 25m NNE of (2) is a sloping outcrop sheet with cups, cups and arcs, and a faint cup and ring (NR 790 970).

4. 12m east of (3) are cups, cups and rings.

5. 5m west of (4) is a large cup and a small cup with an arc.

6. 4m NNE of (4) are three cups in line.

7. 30m NNE of (6) on a prominent rock outcrop are four cups and a cup and ring (NR 790 970).

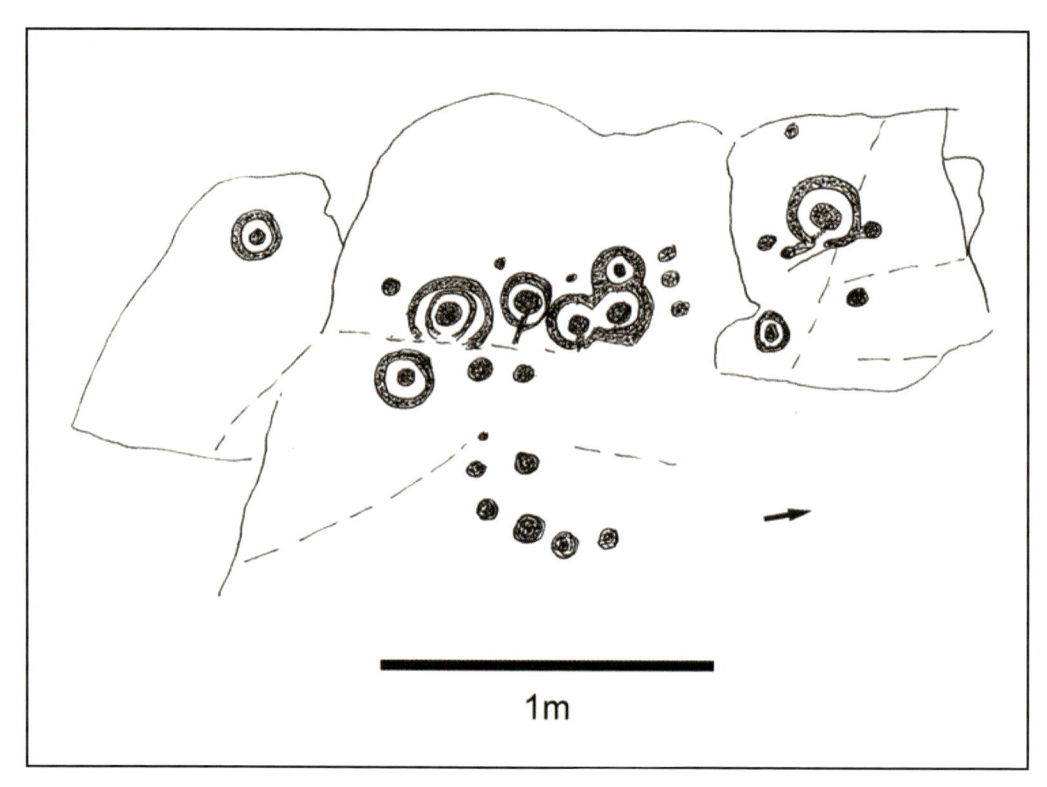

162a. Ardifuir 8

162b. Ardifuir 8

8. 20m NNE of (7) is a larger group of figures including a cup with two rings, seven cups with single rings (four with ducts), a cup and single ring and 20 cups (NR 790 970).

9. Nine cups are on outcrop 50m NNE of (8) at NR 790 971.

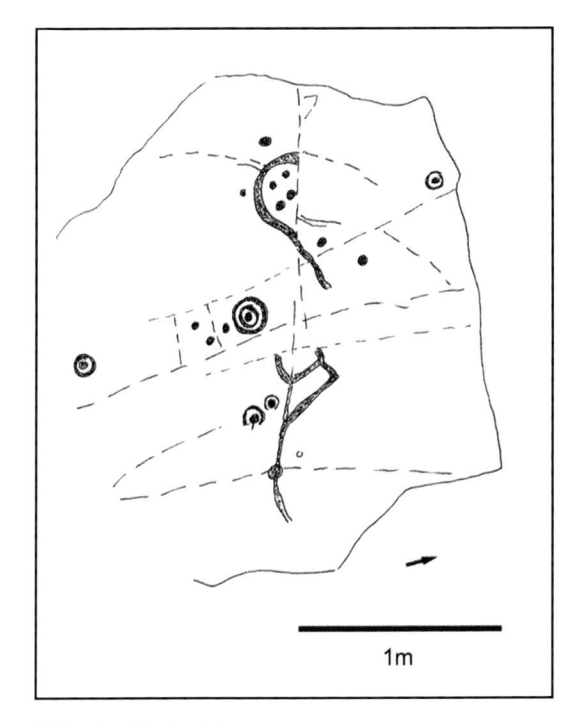

10. On the north flank of the dun, north of the stone wall a rock slope has a cup and two rings, two cups with ducts and single rings, two cups with single rings, 10 cups and two joined cups (NR 788 970).

11. 30m NE of (10) on outcrop are 15 cups, a cup and duct with a ring, and two cups joined with a groove (NR 788 970). There have been other recent finds, reported in 1994 (DES). We have added the numbers to the list above. They are:

12. At NR 770 9722: four cups enclosed by two rings and 28 cups with one ring each. There are 227-250 single cups on a long ridge west of the farmhouse.

13. At NR 7706 9722 there are three possible cups on a projecting outcrop beyond a major gully.

163. Ardifuir 10

14. At NR 7849 9701 there are three cups with one ring each, 51 cups, and four or five 'runnels' on an outcrop ridge that slopes eastward into the ground. Many of the cups are large.

15. At NR 7843 9692 there are 22 cups, some very large, on the same outcrop as the one described above, but lower.

Crinan Ferry (NR 792 936)
There is a lagoon on the west side of the Crinan Canal in which a cup marked boulder was revealed in low water in 1976. This is still visible, but not for close examination; 22 cups were reported on it.

Dun Righ, Eilean Righ (NM 797 010)
This very small island's highest ridge has a dun built on it. To the south is a single cup on the ridge.

9. Loch Awe to Upper Largie

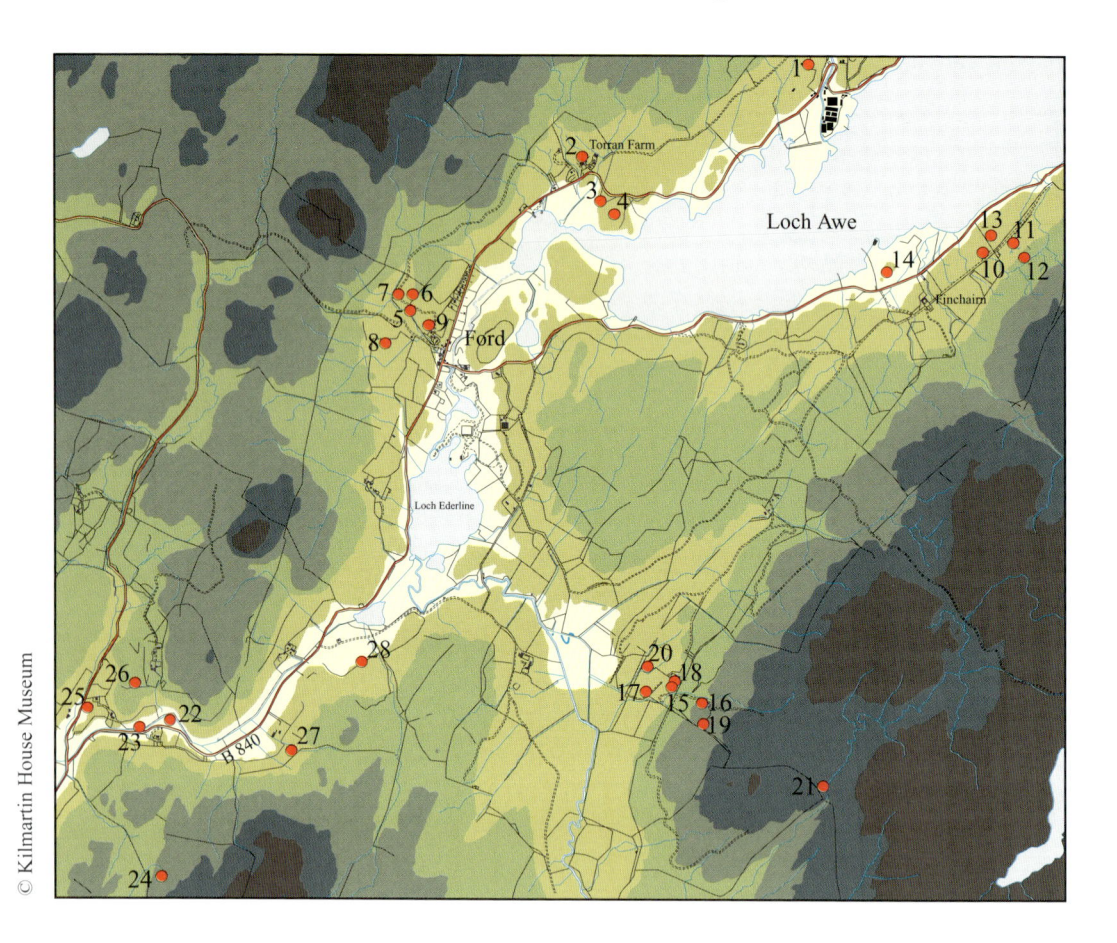

164. Location map of Loch Awe to Upper Largie

1. Inverliever
2. Torran 1
3. Torran 2
4. Torran 4
5. Ford 1 & 2
6. Ford 3
7. Ford 4
8. Ford 5
9. Ford
10. Finchairn 1
11. Finchairn 2
12. Finchairn 3
13. Finchairn 4
14. Finchairn 5
15. Glasvaar 1
16. Glasvaar 2
17. Glasvaar 3
18. Glasvaar 4
19. Glasvaar 5
20. Glasvaar 6
21. Allt Bealaich Ruaidh
22. Eurach 1
23. Eurach 2
24. Eurach 3
25. Creagantairbh 1
26. Creagantairbh 2
27. Glennan
28. Tigh a'Charman

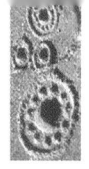

There have been discoveries of rock art on either side of Loch Awe as well as cairns and standing stones at Finchairn, Inverliever and Torran through to Ford, where Loch Awe joins Loch Ederline. At Ford there is a concentration of decorated rock and a large standing stone. The Clachandubh Burn flows into Loch Ederline from the south, overlooked by a decorated outcrop and a cairn at Glasvaar. From here the glen narrows, with standing stones and cairns leading through Eurach to the Kilmartin Burn. Close to this junction, to the north, is a long, decorated outcrop on the edge of Creaganterve Mhor.

Inverliever (NM 983 055)

There is a ruined cottage with the remains of an old wall east of the SE gable. At least three weathered cup marks have been reported on an upright boulder built into the wall.

Torran (NM 879 046)

The site at Torran is on an outcrop that slopes steeply to the water, the slope ending at a small loch that it overlooks, although it is not at the highest point in the landscape.

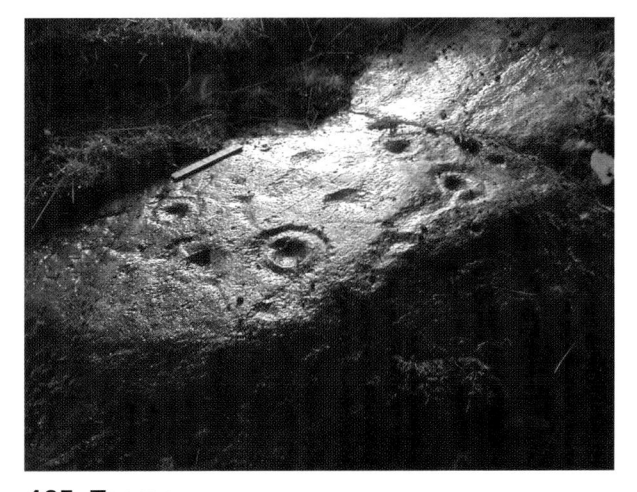

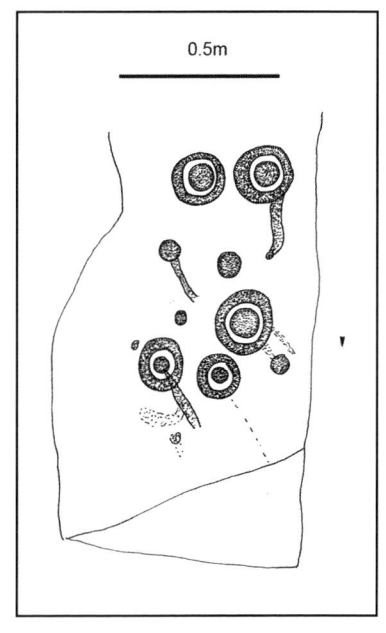

165. Torran

166. Torran

The highest motifs on the south side are two large cups with rings, one having a duct (or tail) coming from the ring. Then there are two cups, one with a duct, a small cup below; and three cups each with a ring. One has a duct running through the ring and one has a cup connected to its ring by a faint, possibly natural groove. All these motifs are very clear in low light, especially when the rock is wet. Nearby is a standing stone at NM 878 048, 3.3m high, with a pecked cross on two faces. One has a cup mark in the right arm of the cross. Another marked rock at NM 803 045 has been reported 100m SE of the crest of the crag. It overlooks Loch Awe and has a single cup (DES 1979).

Ford

Some places appear friendlier than others for all kinds of reasons. Ford has endeared itself to us particularly since we attended a Sunday service in this little village when all the people who came greeted us most cordially. The minister stood in her pulpit, welcomed us heartily and asked us where we came from; this was very much our style, and we responded with equal cordiality. We always have the same kind of reception at the church at Kilmartin, which Barbara and Paul liked so much that they were married there, with the author as best man.

Leading out of Ford village, with its prominent early Bronze Age cairn, is a drove road to Salachary, and there is a group of markings, the first about 11m north of the track.

1. NM 865 038. There is more on this conglomerate outcrop than meets the eye, and the value of a careful rubbing has demonstrated this.

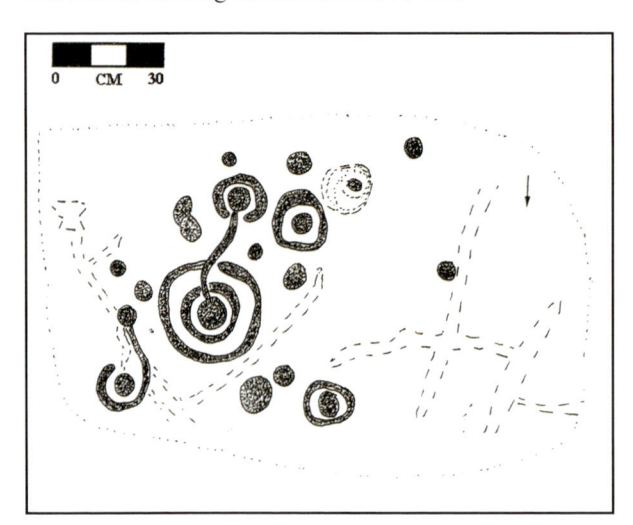

167. Ford 1

Central is a cup as a focus of two concentric penannular rings through which a duct runs from the cup and connects with another cup and penannular to the cup. Spread around these motifs are 11 cups, a cup and arc, two cups and single rings, two joined on contact, and a cup with faint rings. The rock is at an outstanding viewpoint, with the village visible below. Behind it, the land rises to high ground. As with so much else in Argyll, the site was first reported by Marion Campbell, in 1960. The first drawing appeared in Ronald Morris' Argyll book of 1977, but my drawing is somewhat different from his.

2. NM 865 038. NNW of the latter outcrop 45m away north of the highest point of the track is a rock with two cupmarks.

3. NM 865 039. There is an enclosure that has not been excavated, lying below these marked rocks. It is difficult to trace its details, but the circular enclosure is marked by a number of outward facing boulders, the rest being slighted. 35m outside the enclosure to the west is a slab with a faint cup and ring which we were unable to locate.

4. NM 864 039. The 'Dun Dubh Boulder', 35m west of the enclosure, has eight cups and two joined by a groove. It is a partly turf-covered smooth schist boulder. Morris describes a 'part ring 15cm diameter around a probably natural oval basin' and locates it 36m NW of the plantation wall's corner and 120m north of the pine wood's outer wall.

5. NM 864 037. On a boulder that lies south of the track on the west flank of a knoll are eight cups

6. NM 867 038. To the east of these sites there is a well-established planted forest. Close to the track running uphill through it on the village side, is a long outcrop, partly quarried, mostly covered over. RCAHMS was unable to locate this at the time of their survey, and we were only able to locate some of the decoration, drawn here. Ronald Morris and the Ordnance Survey team between 1970 and 1974 were unable to find it, but in 1960 Marion Campbell reported cups and rings in two main groups, including 'two pairs with tangential outer rings'. There is apparently more on this 17.6m long outcrop than we re-located.

The drawing and photograph show a long thin area defined by natural crack lines with well-made cups and cup and rings leading to a cup at the centre of three pear-shaped concentric grooves. Without the forest, the outcrop would be a good viewpoint, and perhaps mark a path from low to high ground. Today, it is located by following the forest track from its principal entrance at the village uphill; the marked rock is buried under leaf mould and needles to the left of the track.

168. Ford 6

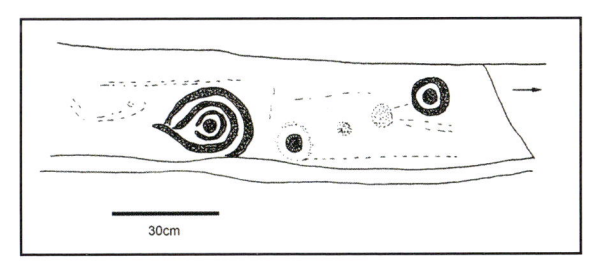

169. Ford 6

Finchairn

170. Finchairn looking north to Loch Awe

From Ford a road (B840) runs eastwards along the south bank of Loch Awe to Finchairn. Much of the bank is wooded with small plantations, and to the south the land rises to A'Chruach and Sidh Mhor, just over 300m. The views across the loch are very attractive. The farm of Finchairn is just south of the road; from it runs a trackway eastward to what used to be a shepherd's house and is now holiday accommodation. This is the focus of some rock art that is mostly made up of cups.

NM 905 042. Before the shepherd's house is reached there is a long ridge of outcrop to the north about 100m WSW of the cottage. Parts have been quarried, but other parts are like an extended table with a straight edge and a fairly uniform top. There are nine widely spaced cup marks on the surface, but all but two were overgrown in 2003.

NM 907 043. 50m NE of the cottage is a gently sloping outcrop, at the NE end of which is a cup and two rings, a cup and duct with two-and-a-half rings, and a cup with a duct and ring. This is now covered over (2003), trampled extensively by cattle.

NM 908 042. The only visible decorated rock surface is about 140m SE of the cottage: a flat outcrop with a knocking stone basin. At least 90 weathered cups are reported there, but it is doubtful whether all are artificial. However the rock is in a commanding position to view the whole sweep of the loch.

Other marked rocks have been reported south of the farmhouse by Kaledon Naddair, but these were covered up at the time of our last visit in 2003. They are all higher up the slope than 1-3, at NR 9060 0435 and NR 8985 0420. The former has 30-40 cups, two with single rings. The latter has nine cups on the edge of outcrop (DES (1961, 8), DES (1972, 11). DES (1973, 13), DES (1994, 50)).

171. Finchairn on a ridge above the cottage, outcrop with over 90 faint cups.

Glasvaar

Glasvaar is the centre of many cup and ring marked outcrops. As a prelude to these, there is a boulder built into the south wall of the farmhouse, exposed on the north side of the road (NM 884 014). It is a fluid design of many grooves, linking cups, an oval, and three cups with single rings.

172. Glasvaar farm wall, a built-in decorated boulder

173. Glasvaar wall boulder

The most important group of motifs lies on a whaleback of outcrop that runs NE from the farm, providing a high viewpoint and the route of a hollow way. There is a large knocking stone basin in this rock that may have carried a way-marker post, from which the route moves downhill to a stream glen. The whaleback is on two levels, with decoration on both. The higher has its decoration visible today, running roughly north to south with multiple cups, six cups with single rings, a cup and arc, a cup joined to another, and three cups with small ducts (NM 885 019).

174. Glasvaar: a line of boulders leading to decorated outcrop.

More dramatic and complex are the motifs on a lower level, now grassed over. At the north end there is a cup and ring at the centre of six concentric arcs and an additional seventh that is not quite so long, ending in a cup. This motif has seven cups on its south side, hemmed in by a natural crack. Above it are five small concentric arcs containing one or two cups in each above the crack. Below them is an occulus of an elaborate design: two cups and single rings separated by a cup, with the whole enclosed by a figure-of-eight groove. There is another occulus further south made up of two touching cups and rings. The southern part is very 'busy' with interconnected cups and rings and cups that are clustered in a line.

109

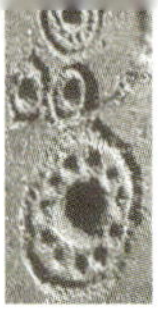

South east of this (NM 886 018) 70m away is an outcrop with motifs interconnected with grooves and a unique pair of cups with single rings joined by three parallel grooves, the whole enclosed by an oval.

6.5m further east of this are four cups on an outcrop.

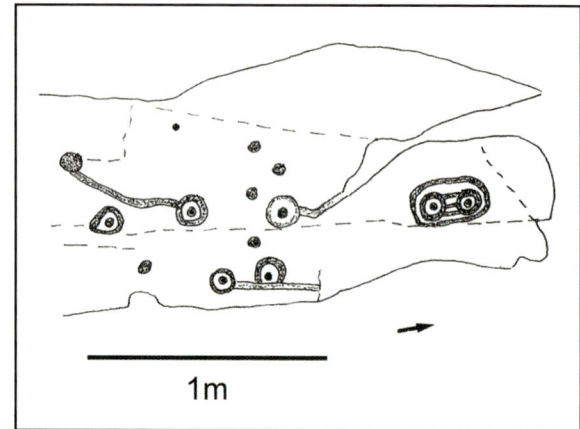

175. The only exposed part of the ridge today.

176. A secondary outcrop

New sites have been found recently around the farmhouse. A boulder with 15 cups rests on an outcrop, which is also cup marked (NM 882 013).

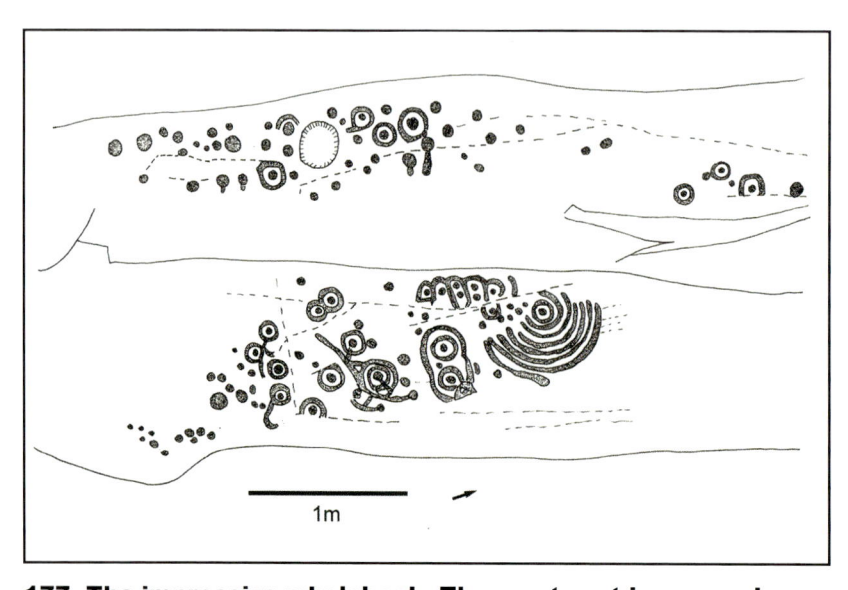

177. The impressive whaleback. The east part is covered over

110

At NM 884 014 south of the wall with the boulder in it are two cups on an outcrop sheet. Kaledon Naddair has found sheets of outcrop covered with cups and cups and rings, but these were covered over since excavation and are not available for examination (DES 1992 Naddair). The following are his discoveries and numbers:

NM 886 013. A large outcrop on a hill slope above and SE of the farm, bared of turf, revealed 107 cups and 13 with one ring each.

NM 882 014. On bedrock below a well-known cup marked boulder were three clear cups. Glasvaar today is a remote and rather isolated area, but there are hollow ways that suggest a frequent route across high ground.

Allt Bealaich Ruaidh (NM 894 007)

This site is one of the most remote. It lies high on the moorland on the north east fringes of planted forest about 1.2km SE of Glasvaar. The rock sheet is situated on the north bank of the stream, and its position there may have been significant to mobile people who watered their animals in this high ground in the summer. Although the motifs have weathered, there are two cups with ducts and rings, a cup with two rings, four cups with rings and four cups (RCAHMS).

Eurach (NM 848 010)

Eurach lies close to the confluence of this glen with the Kilmartin Burn. Close to a shepherd's house on outcrops are two groups of cupmarks. One is on a level surface of a boss overlooking a cliff immediately north of Eurach with at least 30 cups, some linked by grooves, two cups in a pecked oval enclosure, and some recent initials. 5.5m east is a large cup, and 6m to the SW are nine cups on a rock spine (RCHAMS). North of the Ford road is a boulder with two cups at NM 847 011. At NM 849 001 four plain cups were reported on an isolated outcrop (DES 1994. 50).

Creagantairbh (NM 843 012)

178. Creagantairbh: the whole rock from the NE.

This is the last major rock panel north of Kilmartin before the road makes its winding, narrow way up and down hill before the land opens out at Kintraw. It is just north of the glen that opens out to Ford to the east, and the perched boulder on its southern corner is visible from the main road.

The large outcrop, partly turf-covered, lying in pasture, is divided into rectangles by a crack. What can be seen on it depends sometimes how far animals have scraped off some of the grass. The south part has cups and cups and rings spread thinly over its surface; its most interesting part is the NE on a section defined by natural cracks. There is a large oval with a cup in one corner; between this and the edge of the outcrop is a series of small enclosures formed by a network of grooves. A long groove leads out of these motifs, the furthest extent of the marking.

At the centre of the rectangle is a large deep cup with an ungapped ring. There are three other smaller cups with a single ring. Some cups are in lines, two are touching, and two are connected by a groove.

The western rectangle is more crowded with motifs, mainly well-made cups, some with grooves and some joined, and four deep cups each surrounded by an ungapped ring. To the north is a smaller countersunk cup at the centre of a ring that includes a small cup. To the east are two small cups with faint single rings.

At NM 844 012 SE of this outcrop on the highest point are two cups (RCAHMS). At NM 8469 0137 a loose boulder with at least one cup, and worn cups on a smaller earthfast boulder at its foot were reported (DES 1994, 50). A cist was found on arable land somewhere in the region of NM 8501, but it was reburied.

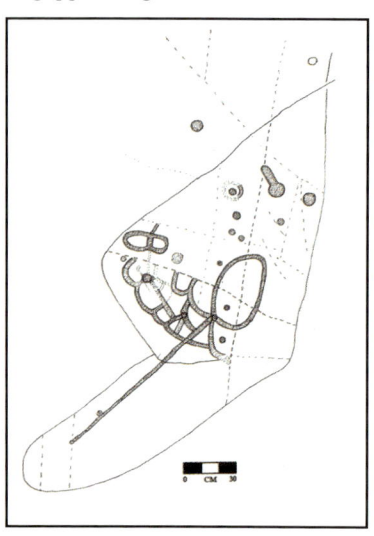

180. The NE end

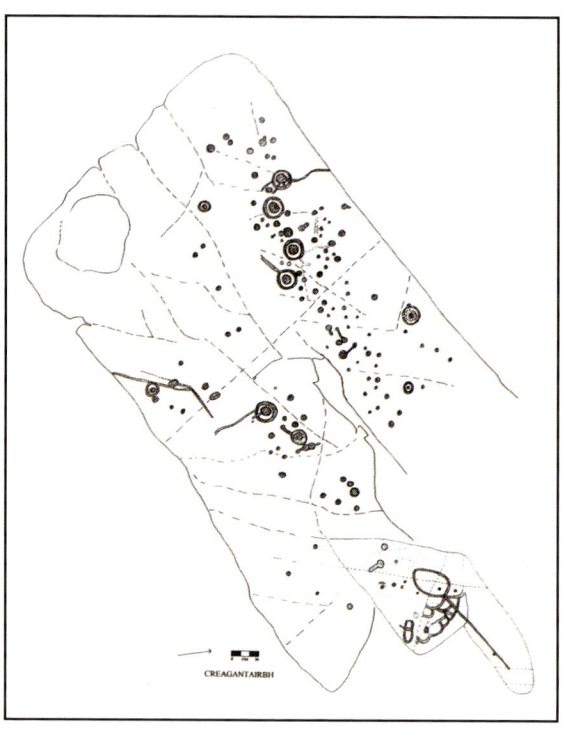

179. Creagantairbh the whole rock

181. The NE end

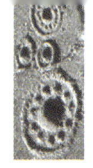

10. Kilbride

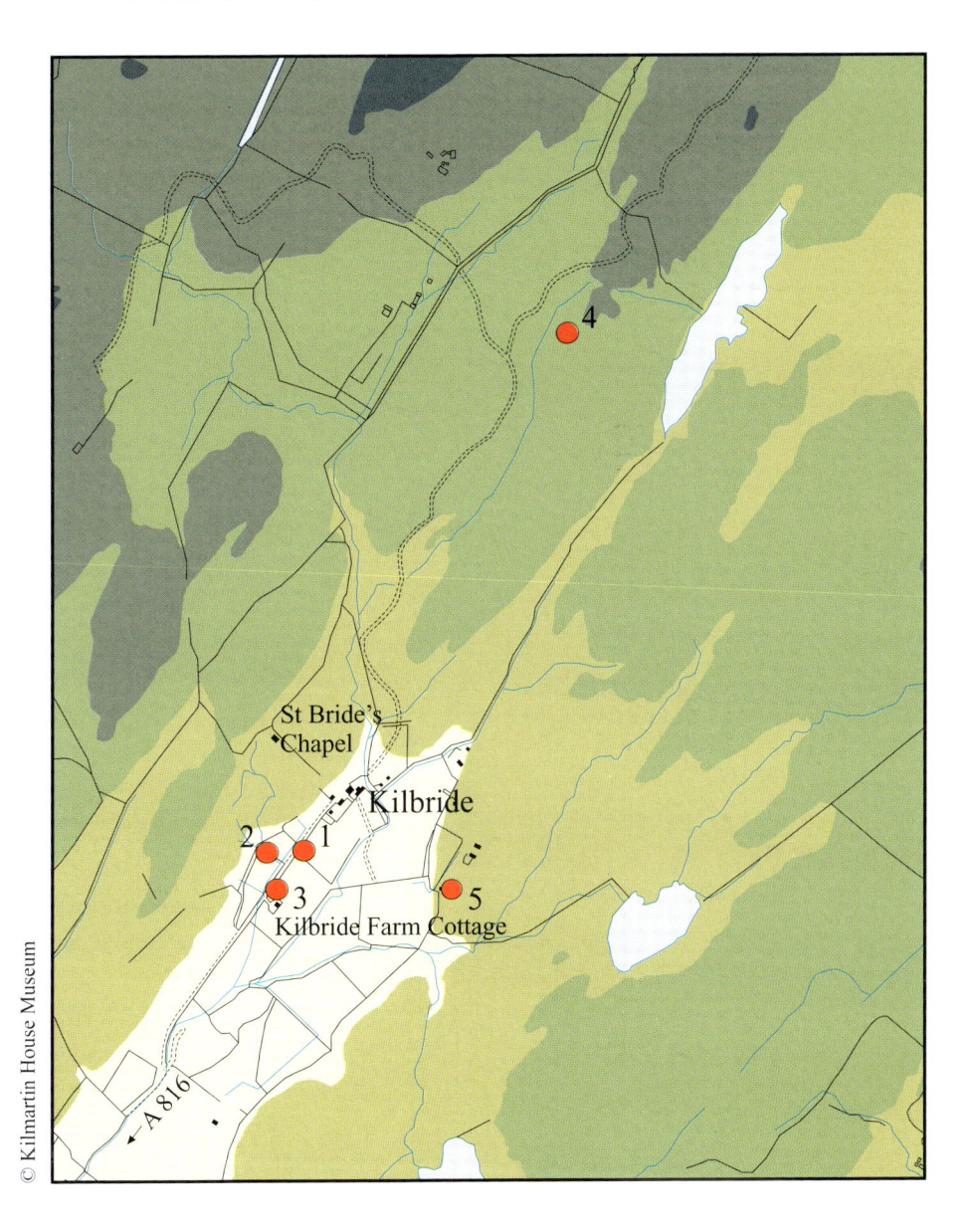

182. Location Plan of Kilbride

1. Kilbride 1-4
2. Kilbride 5
3. Kilbride 6-8
4. Kilbride 9
5. Kilbride 10

Parallel to the glens already described, where rock art follows the course of their streams to lead to the Kilmartin Burn and the River Add is the glen from Loch Add, through Kilbride and Rhudle Mill to Anaskeog. There are a chambered cairn and other cairns on either side of this glen. The rock art is found on a low spine of rock that runs SW along the glen from Kilbride Farmhouse. The motifs are cups and cups and rings, found in groups. Two on a boulder lie in the farm garden and are only available for inspection with permission from people who live there. The others lie beside the road in pasture, but are obscured by grass.

183. Kilbride: outcrop with simple cups overlooking the widest part of the glen in the NE.

184. Kilbride: simple motifs on outcrop on the glen floor south of the road to the farm.

1. NR 852 964. The motifs in the garden begin at the highest part of the outcrop with four cups by the SE garden wall, then two cups and a cup and two rings. This part of the outcrop is about 220m long.
2. NR 852 964. Close to the NW garden wall on the outcrop ridge are 70 cups and the basin of a knocking-stone.
3. NR 852 964. A boulder with a cup and two rings, cup and ring, three cups and a cup with a groove was moved from its position in a ploughed field (NR 8503 9593) to the garden and is next to (2)
4. NR 852 964. 55m west of (2) in a field and 10m from the field wall is an outcrop with two cups and single rings and three cups.
5. NR 851 964. About 60m SW of (4) is an outcrop with a triangular setting of three large cups, two of which have single rings and the other with an arc. Two other cups lie inside the triangle and one on the outside.
6. NR 851 963. 35m SW of (5) are two groups of five and three cups.
7. NR 851 963. 300m SE of the farmhouse are two decorated erratic boulders on the floor of the valley. One has a cup and the other has two cups.

8. NR 8512 9632. On a continuation of the main outcrop rock six cups each enclosed by a ring, and 23 cups have been reported (DES 1994, 50).

9. NR 859 977 (Campbell, PSAS 95). A flat boulder was reported at Crubagean in a wide marshy gully overlooking the Kilbride Glen, sunk into the slope at the NE. It has more than 30 cups, with at least one group arranged as a rosette. Miss Campbell said that the local name may mean a toad or a small crouching thing. A local report called it a 'Covenantor's Communion Table with hollows for the cups'.

Once again we see the rock art following a valley route leading to the concentration of monuments between Dunamuck and Baluachraig.

10. NR 855 963. An outcrop next to a wood has cup marks (see illustration 184)

11. The East coast
The eastern limit of the area has two sites of rock art.

Barr (NR 968 953)
A small metalled road that leads off the A83 to Barr house passes an outcrop to the west, set in a well-kept lawned area. The rock terrace has a cup and three rings, a duct leading to a cup with an arc and three cups. The view from the top of the outcrop over Loch Fyne is impressive.

Brainport Bay (NR 975 951)
Our first visit to this site in May 2003 was through a very attractive wood fringed with an impressive and interesting coastline. Mossed walls, bluebells, varied trees and barnacle-covered rocks made the approach to this site from the north a great visual experience that continued on the route back to the road via Minard Castle.

A setting of stone platforms and possible standing stones that were excavated recently at NR 975 951 now has its own display board to describe what was found and (perhaps more controversially) what it was used for. Close to the sea above the level of the raised beach is a platform with a small rectangular extension constructed of slabs and boulders and covered with quartz fragments that include flint flakes, a core and a pointed implement. SW of the platform is an earthen bank 50m long and 3m thick that produced a prehistoric date from underneath. About 70m behind the SW platform is another, with a group of boulders in between, one 2m high, nearest the sea (called the 'terraces and causeway'). The main platform is D-shaped, constructed with a kerb of boulders, 9.5m across, with two smaller platforms attached. A recumbent stone found there has been re-erected. Whatever the original intention of the platforms, thought by some for aligning standing stones, there is evidence of industrial activity including iron working. Quartz and flint implements give the site an earlier, prehistoric use. Its importance emphasises the significance of two cup marked rocks nearby, at NR 975 951. They are about 50m from the coast, in the planted forest, NW of the site just described. A low outcrop under a tree has two cups.

There is a rock sheet with many cups on its undulating surface. Just as the platform site shows later activity, this one was used for the manufacture of quern stones, as our photograph shows. We could find no reference to it. It is possible that the rock art and a phase in the construction of the platforms are contemporary, as the discovery of flint and quartz suggests. That the same site was chosen by groups of prehistoric people is of great significance. Access to the sea may have been one reason, but there may be others unknown to us.

Sron-na-Bruil (NR 95928 93493)

On the Minard estate a stone was found by Mr J.Bell and reported on the Canmore website by P.F. Gladwin in 1992. I have made an accurate drawing of this large glaciated boulder that lies in planted forest about 100m from Loch Fyne in a grassy clearing. It is covered with cups and cups and rings. Another has been reported further south at East Kames, so it is interesting to see the spread of discoveries closer to the sea.

185. Brainport cup-marked stone.

186. Millstone quarrying on the cup-marked rock.

187. Sron-na-Bruil 3

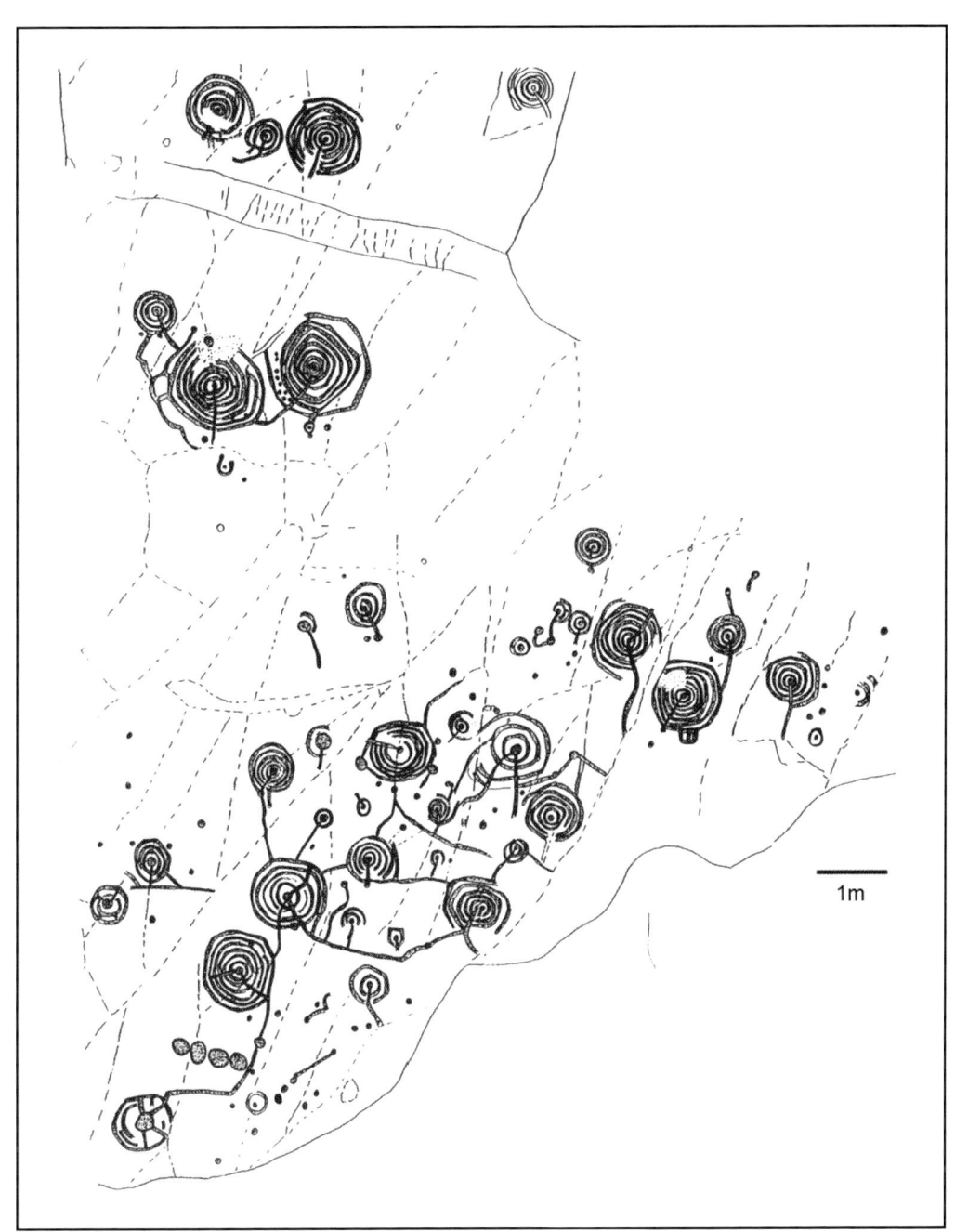

188. Achnabreck: to conclude this survey, this large decorated outcrop is a reminder of the complexity and skill of Kilmartin rock art.

12. The significance of the distribution of Rock Art in the region and its wider context

The Kilmartin area is in many ways a microcosm of rock art studies in Britain. The geographical area is well defined and varied. Marked rocks in the open air are numerous and are distributed in such a way that it is possible to infer some sort of logic from their distribution. It is clear from the pick marks how the motifs were made. The arrangement of symbols has produced many variations in style and complexity.

Although the dating of open-air rock art is impossible as yet, there is a strong link between motifs and monuments that gives us some idea of chronology, but nothing absolute. The unique presence of cup marks and outlines of metal axes in cists at least gives us a 'final' date for their use. The concentration of burials, monuments, standing stones and stone circles shows the importance of this area to prehistoric people and includes some 'diagnostic' artefacts (tools that are distinctive and identified with a certain period and people), pottery and jewellery. The area has some special characteristics too: the use of jointed cist side slabs, unique in the British Isles, and the inclusion in cists of two stones decorated with lines instead of circles and curves.

The history of the exploration of British rock art has a special place, too, for it was here that the antiquarians identified this special contribution to our knowledge of prehistory. It added a language of signs to a non-literary culture. The story of their discoveries and speculations has been added to since then, yet despite the increase in information, we still ask similar questions, and still await answers. We must always keep a sense of proportion: as with so much in the past, we have probably lost a great amount, and tend to make generalisations from what is left. If rock art has been used over at least a thousand years, we have a tiny representation to scatter over that period, like a little sand on a lawn. The sum total of what we know has to be examined carefully and added to our knowledge of rock art in the rest of Britain and indeed in the rest of the world.

In attempting some sort of synthesis, many questions must be asked. Will the collection of more data enable archaeologists to draw conclusions about what the motifs mean, or do we already have sufficient information to make a judgement? Are we further along the road to understanding than the antiquarians of the 19th century who became fascinated by the phenomenon?

Does my knowledge of so many areas and detailed familiarity with the panels and single marked stones put me in a better position than anyone else to offer a hypothesis? Am I aware of the significance of what I already know? Do the insights that I have gained from a variety of sources enable me to deal with the relationships between the types of motifs made, the landscapes where they occur and the contexts of burials and monuments where some of them are found? How much of my cultural background will help or get in the way of understanding something of the minds of people who lived over 4000 years ago?

Is there a danger of transferring knowledge of other cultures that used symbols as paintings, etchings and pecked-out designs on rock surfaces to those of northern Britain? How far is analogy useful and how far misleading? How far can developments in disciplines related to archaeology such as science, aesthetics, psychology and philosophy help us to understand rock art? Changes in emphasis in all these disciplines, refutation of one idea and substitution by another should warn us that our own conclusions will certainly be questioned, but that we must make the effort to hypothesise and open ourselves up to the challenge now or in the future.

In studying rock art we are drawn deeply into motives for human behaviour thousands of years ago. The spread, context and frequency of motifs alert us to their importance in the prehistoric world. The fact that 'geometric' shapes rather than pictures of people and animals are exclusive subjects tells us that something is being taken out of the 'natural' world and represented in a powerful kind of shorthand. The process of abstracting such important symbols comes from the mind either through observation of something in nature or from some deep-rooted, built-in imagery. Consciousness or awareness of the world does not come merely by observing it and living in it or by using intelligence to solve problems. Strong feelings play an important part in the way we think and how we perceive the world. The mind can be heightened by excitement, and we learn and create not just in a state of cold reason but by stimulation. In our dreams a world partly 'real' and a world created and imaginary comes to the surface; their revelations can be very disturbing and evoke many of our anxieties. The apparently simplest of human emotions are the most difficult to articulate, and poets may choose analogy to create 'layers of meaning'. Words themselves arranged in a pattern produce sounds that not merely convey meaning but also some of the feeling that gives rise to that meaning so that it can be strongly expressed. It is possible to understand a poem without knowing exactly what it means. Perhaps the poet doesn't know either, otherwise it might have been written in another way, such as prose. The writer may not be fully conscious of the implications of everything that has been written, and the reader or listener may get something from it that is unique to him or her.

There are thousands of images that we live with daily that are more general and perhaps more widely shared. A road sign, National Trust oak leaves, National Parks curlew, Boy Scout fleur de lis are common enough in England, and the thistle in Scotland, but not all people recognise a curlew or know why a lily flower and clover have become the symbols of Guides and Scouts. Yet we can all know what they stand for generally without knowledge of how they originated. A crescent, cross, star of David, red cross, green cross mean different things to people in different countries. During the Crusades for example, feeling was such that when the cross and the crescent met there was slaughter. We are familiar with images that are pictorial, such as a steam train at a crossing, children walking to school, danger of falling rocks – warnings without words.

In prehistoric art 'pictures' of animals, places and human activities may carry far more meaning to the people who made them and to those who saw them than to us. When cave paintings were first discovered in Europe they were so vivid that people at first refused to believe that they could possibly be so old; they had preconceived ideas that 'savages' were incapable of such art. This idea has changed; those who painted such images in caves are now thought by some to have done so when they had trance visions through which they acquired the images that they depicted, so that animals took on a much greater significance than something to be hunted and eaten. The idea of people painting such images because they had plenty of time to do so was also rejected along with the concept of 'art for art's sake'. This type of art was fundamental to a whole view of life that was so important that it was expressed in dangerous, narrow and confined spaces underground where perhaps only a few people would ever see it, and only with the help of lights carried down there.

The 'meaning' of such images continues to be explored with questions such as: why are there so many dots? What characteristics of the animals are singled out specially, and why? Were they made by people with special powers and perceptions? Were such perceptions rooted firmly in human brains since *Homo sapiens* emerged? How were such perceptions brought from the depths to the surface of human minds? What did it all mean?

Having established that people who lived thousands of years ago were capable of expressing their perceptions of the real and spirit world so vividly in their art, this capability is certainly possible amongst any group of humans in the world, and certainly in Neolithic Britain. If we view cup and ring art with this in mind, and give prehistoric people credit for coming to terms not only with survival in a hunting and farming world, they are also to be credited with being 'spiritual beings'. Many of their greatest buildings are non-functional, non-domestic in that they were not built to store things in or to live in. Stone circles and henges were community centres, a focus for scattered farmers who felt the need to keep together periodically to establish a tribal identity through chat, trade, and by sharing a life that involved ritual. Some of the standing stones of these structures were decorated with cups, cups and rings and spirals.

The way they disposed of the dead suggests a ritual and a sense of continuity in a spirit world after death. The Irish passage graves point in no uncertain terms to the use of symbols and motifs in profusion in something like a man-made cave, full of darkness and mystery. Although the kerbstones surrounding the great mounds carry simple and complex decoration, it is the interior, reached through passages, where a special and awesome place is constructed. Newgrange may have had some of the feeling taken out of it by being made presentable for an enquiring and eager public, but it is still a powerful experience. More powerful still is a visit to the Loughcrew sites where there is no electric light and only 'darkness visible' in a passage grave where I found myself surrounded by a remarkable array of symbols woven into designs. It was, quite frankly, frightening. Many have the same reaction to the restored mound of Maes Howe on Orkney. Having to crawl along a narrow, low tunnel to reach the main chamber is a preparation for this underworld experience.

The Irish passage graves have decoration that seems so profuse that, compared with what is seen in the open air, it seems extreme. Imagine taking the Christian cross and covering it with jewels and multiple decorations, compared with the simple wayside crosses on a pilgrim route. The passage graves of the Boyne valley are the strongest statement in Britain of the power of place and symbol in prehistoric times. There is also a great sense of continuity there. Seamus Heaney, for example, in his poem 'Funeral Rites', takes the site at Newgrange as a place where all human feeling and thought about the dead can be focused in a ritual now as in the past (Heaney 1990).

Monuments and burials link rock art with 'religion' to a ritual involving the dead. That ritual is not all-inclusive as it is possible that the 'specialised' use of certain physical areas in the mounds was only accessible by a limited number of people. It has been so ever since, in all kinds of religious buildings. Control in religion is power. Monuments to the dead in churches or churchyards in Britain hardly acknowledge that death is a leveller, for their size and ostentation implies a glory and status beyond death. The rich and influential go on expressing the belief that they will remain so in the next world. Some people inherit power and some take it. Silver floats to the surface leaving the lead below in the refining fire.

Buried motifs pose all sorts of questions. Are such motifs specially developed from simpler ones because their function becomes more important? The sense of place that we have when we visit these graves and ritual centres is dependent not only on the constructions themselves but also on their settings. Castlerigg in Cumbria is a stone circle at the centre of a circle of mountains; a place that already lifts the spirit before the stones and their markings begin to affect us. Long Meg towers over the other stones in the circle at the entrance to the circle, detached from them, possibly older, decorated on the whole of one face that looks to the centre of the circle.

Of course the next question about graves and monuments is why they are not all decorated with cup and ring motifs and spirals. A few cups and rings have appeared in the south of England, but they are almost negligible. Were these motifs common on materials such as wood and cloth? Were they painted or tattooed on human skin? We don't know. Why were so few burials chosen to incorporate rock art? Is this because the archaeological record is so patchy rather than its being a true picture of distribution? Why do Stonehenge and Kilmartin have the only axe motifs?

At least there is a period of use to be deduced when art is found in burial and monumental contexts. We can attribute it to a broad time-scale from about 3000-2000BC. We can surmise that it had something to do with how monuments were used and how the dead were buried, but most British rock art is in the

189. Stonehenge : stone 53 in 1973

landscape, so what purpose did the motifs serve there? Although there seems to be a stronger link establishing the period of use and possible reasons for use in burials and monuments, the logic for its distribution in the landscape is clearer than many have supposed. There are now thousands of recorded marked rocks and an analysis of locations should help us understand why they exist where they do. Hundreds have been destroyed, but there should be sufficient data to make some intelligent suggestions.

One of the first archaeologists to put the distribution of marked rocks in the landscape into some sort of coherent order was Richard Bradley, working with a team of students that could do the fieldwork on a large scale. At the beginning of his book (Bradley 1997) on the results of his investigations he stresses the importance of theory. We observe something in the landscape, something is revealed, and we ask questions about it. We form a theory, but the next step is to work hard at finding what brought us to that theory in the first place. It is a leap of imagination that must be traced back to psyche and experience. We have to find a method to assess the value of our interpretations, and this requires discipline.

Bradley gives an example of how this procedure worked in his awakened interest in rock art, when a visit to Ilkley Moor 'set one wondering just how such places had been used'. He began with the idea that the rocks are 'signs', places in the landscape that gave information, and would have had meanings for the people there. That applies to any rock art area in Britain, for just by walking the routes from one panel to another gives a sense of markers being offered, without our being able to understand what those particular symbols mean. Whereas archaeology relies on such things as settlements and artefacts for an understanding of people, a different approach was needed here because the element of mobility had to be taken into account. People whose lives depend entirely or partially on moving around the landscape cannot afford to clash with other groups, and need to define their areas of special interest. Perhaps marking the rocks with their signs would do this. The more dependent people were (farming in one place, with defined fields for crops and pasture, and living areas), the less mobile their lives; although they would still need to leave the settlement to hunt, or to lead livestock to fresh pasture. These hunting and pasture areas, outside the most fertile arable lands, would have been on what we call 'marginal' land, not the best for arable farming, but still rich in food. In Northumberland, around the fertile Milfield plain, where the ritual monuments lie and where the best arable land is, are sandstone scarps that Clive Waddington sees as 'inscribed' grazing areas defined by cup and ring marks (Waddington 1998). The same marginal areas also include most burial cairns, mostly of the late Neolithic/early Bronze Age type. If rock art defines areas of grazing for one group, then such areas may be crossed or be linked by trails, as beasts do not graze in one spot. Some archaeologists believe that the decline in use of rock motifs was the result of a decline in the mobility of prehistoric peoples, and this has been used for suggesting a very early date for rock art: more settled farming reducing the need to mark rocks. There is no reason why mobile grazing should decline because of settled farming; hunting and pasture continued to be essential, especially as populations and demand for food increased.

Bradley states that mainstream archaeology has missed out something significant by not seeing mobility as important, and instead of seeing rock art as 'a medium for wider study of prehistoric society and its occupation of the landscape' they have treated rock art in the same way as portable artefacts. He asks what rock art was actually advertising? What information was it giving? Whatever answers may come from this, one may be sure that we have no means of knowing exactly what it meant. As it was used over such a considerable period of time, it is even unlikely the people who made the motifs were aware of how the whole process began. That does not mean that people went through some meaningless and outdated ritual when they made the marks. They must have known that what they were doing was important and of great significance. We use words without thinking about how they came into being or of what they are composed. We use symbols in everyday life without thinking about why they were chosen to mean what they mean. The fact that the motifs are abstract does not help us to understand them; such motifs may hold many meanings for the people who made and understood them, like 'layers of meaning' in poetry. Not only that, but also the meaning of the images may have changed over time.

If we accept that whatever we do we may not be able to crack the code, we are faced with the more profitable task of trying to find a logic to their distribution in the landscape. There are plenty of data that enable us to make distribution maps. We can place sites and single marked rocks precisely on a map, draw diagrams to show their height above sea level, find out what kind of rock they are pecked on and whether they are related in their distribution to various types of soil. Richard Bradley and his group recorded for the first time how far away one has to be before a rock becomes visible; conclusion: close by. He worked out what can be seen from a rock, and demonstrated that very many of them command wide views in different directions (allowing for whatever vegetation might have been in the way at the time, such as trees). He noted that many of them overlook valleys and the entrances to plains. He noted clusters of marked rocks in a limited area, and wondered whether this meant that people congregated there at special times. He decided that if we can't know what they mean, at least we may attempt to show 'that they were organised according to certain conventions'.

One of the things that has resulted from my own extensive fieldwork and that of my friends is an instinct about where to look for new rock art, for through this we have discovered many new sites. This hunch can hardly be blind instinct, for we have learnt about places, about rock types, about topography. This is possibly the application of prehistoric logic in deciding where rock art might or ought to be.

A starting point in the search for new marked rocks is in areas where they already have been found. It is rather like finding one flint flake in a ploughed field; it directs attention to the possibility or probability of finding more. Richard Bradley's surveys, not aimed at finding new sites, nevertheless found no new rock art. Yet some people have an uncanny instinct for finding totally new ones. Why? Diligence and interest, of course, and prior knowledge – but some other sense seems to be at work. Very high places are out, and intensively ploughed areas are not usually forthcoming, but the marginal intermediate higher ground is where we find them. Within an established rock art area, the surprises and delights of discovery are our reward. In Northumberland one of the most spectacular recent finds was on the floor of a rock shelter at Ketley Crags. The shelter was in a minor Fell Sandstone cliff that fell away to a stream valley. The most that it could have afforded was a temporary small shelter for two or three people, huddled together, yet the floor has some of the most skilful use of the natural floor as a base for intricate rock art as any we have ever encountered. The significance of the place could not have been just as a shelter, for other rock overhangs would have proved more effective. Can we really say why it was singled out? There is other rock art on the higher ground above it, some of very high quality. The view from the overhang is so widespread and spectacular – over the valley to the distant Cheviot Hills – that its location as a commanding spot must have been one reason for its choice. Could other rocks along the same outcrop have been used? Probably yes, so we may have to acknowledge that other factors were at work in making a choice, and the level of artistry made it even more special. As a meeting place for special occasions it might not have been very suitable as it is on a rather awkward slope. There is a much more suitable dome of rock above it, with rock art that is good, but not as impressive as this.

We can expect patterns to emerge now, but must be prepared for something to challenge our expectations. However, we can make some generalisations about where people placed their motifs.

In Kilmartin, Tayside and a part of Northumberland the bulk of rock art occupies high places that overlook lower ground, bordering and overlooking a loch, surrounding and overlooking a long flat valley, and forming an area of low hills around a flat plain. The pattern is also one that follows rivers and stream courses. Rivers and streams give access to the land, and provide essential water for animals. Rock art also marks the actual sources of streams. On Gales Moor in Richmondshire (Beckensall 1998, 35) one set of cups and linked grooves is uncharacteristically without a view, but draws attention to the spring that they mark. In Howgill, County Durham, (Beckensall 1998, 82), a flat field has a flat marked rock that lies at the beginning of several springs. At Eels Hill on Barningham Moor (Beckensall 1998, 55) rock art surrounds a major spring source. These are just a few of many examples.

These examples alone show how rock art 'socialises' landscapes, imprinting human signs at specific places. There were already landscape features that would allow travellers, distant or local, to know where they were in their journey; cliffs, large boulders, certain trees would be familiar because they are outstanding. Rock art is lower key; it takes an existing rock surface, studies its form, and begins to use natural indentations, cracks and the shape of the rock itself to produce a design based on simple symbols. In a way this enhances the landscape, humanising it. In what could have appeared as a dangerous wilderness it would have been reassuring. I find that this is my reaction when I find a new decorated panel. It is familiar, yet different, for every rock is different. Beyond the excitement of making a new discovery, it generates a warmth of familiarity for me. It increases my sense of wonder, links me with a past that I only sense in part. If the area itself were unknown to me – as Tayside used to be until quite recently - the very existence of rock art made me feel at home; so much so that I am convinced that prehistoric people visiting that area would have felt the same reassurance. It does not matter how long ago the decoration was made – hundreds, thousands of years ago; it spoke of continuity and reinforced a common identity. People were leaving behind something of themselves, and this was intentionally permanent when rocks are worked on with mallet and pick. We find them, record them, preserve them, try to place them in context and sequence. We follow a gut reaction and attempt to devise a method to understand it; we look beyond our own countries to others where rock art appears to see what can be learnt there. We ask: What compelled them to do it? Who in society made them – a selected few, perhaps?

There are statistical methods that can be applied to the study. Here are some examples:

1. Where are all the known panels of rock art? Map their locations, using GPS to plot them accurately.
2. What can be seen from them; and from how far away can they be seen?
3. What is the nature of the rocks with markings? Sedimentary, metamorphic, igneous? Given a choice, which rocks are favoured?
4. Are there other surfaces suitable for rock art that have not been used? Why were some rocks chosen and not others?
5. Were the 'best' surfaces chosen (i.e. the smoothest and most accessible)? If not, why was an 'unsuitable' rock chosen? Was its surface shape such that it suggested a design, and were its irregularities incorporated? Did the irregularities determine the design? Was the rock at a special place, perhaps where something important had happened?
6. Are there signs that markings were made at different times on the same rock surface? Are there superimpositions? Are there signs that designs could have been re-cut?
7. What kind of symbols/motifs appear on the rocks?
8. How are these markings arranged, related to each other, and spread?
9. With a range from simple to complex (by modern aesthetic judgement), is there a pattern in which more complex motifs appear in different areas or at different heights? Do some combinations of symbols appear in special contexts? If we discover repeated designs, is there any logic to their distribution?

These are useful leading questions, but what has been missing until now is the relationship between where the rock art appears and other archaeology. This relationship should take into account all known information such as:

1. Settlements, including fields and domestic sites
2. Scatters of flint, chert and agate left by temporary settlers.

3. Defensive enclosures
4. Artefact finds
5. Monuments
6. Burials
7. Route-ways

The basic motifs in Britain have already been introduced in Chapter 1. Most panels of rock art and single marking in Kilmartin have been listed, pictured and described, but it remains to study the distribution of these motifs as a whole. The extent of markings on any rock surface must be taken into account. This may depend on what was covered by vegetation in prehistoric times, or in some cases the decoration was framed by leaving a space around it at the edge of the rock. A good example of this is at Ballygowan. In other cases, such as Achnabreck east, only the upper part of the surface is marked, so the lower might have been covered with growth.

A distinction must be drawn between what appears to be a random scatter of symbols from a deliberate design. The problem is that a single cup mark could have been as significant in its context as a more complex design. The modern viewer may be more impressed by size and variety. Some archaeologists have distinguished cups and cups with single rings as 'simple' motifs, and others with multiple rings as 'complex', yet a pattern of cup marks arranged in lines, rosettes or dominoes can be equally 'complex'. However, as a general rule the addition of many rings does seem to produce a more arresting display than a single ring, without our knowing what the addition of extra rings actually meant. Some have considered the possibility of rings being added over a period of time, but there is no evidence for this.

There is a similarity throughout Britain in design elements. Thus rings without a central cup are rarer than rings and a groove centred on a cup. This sameness is broken by features like rosettes, or cups of different sizes joined with a groove (as at Kilmichael Glassary). The spiral breaks away from the usual. Squares and other angular enclosures are very rare.

The most striking differences appear when we consider relationships between the design elements on a rock. These always take into account the natural form of the rock in its slope, surface smoothness or otherwise, the presence of natural cracks or glacial grooves. Natural and artificial are brought together. Direction of slope determines how much sun the rock surface receives at different times of the year, and shadows play an important part in revealing what has been pecked onto the rock. We look at the pattern from the lower slope upwards, but can stand above the design and look around to see what areas of landscape are encompassed from there. What appear to us to be the most sophisticated designs (and therefore the most satisfying aesthetically) are interrelated motifs. Some run into each other or touch. Ducts running from cups may run parallel. Motifs are enclosed singly, or in groups, by cracks. It is this grouping of symbols and motifs that produces 'complex' art.

Is there a regional characteristic in Argyll? Not really, for all that can be seen here is paralleled in the rest of Britain. For example, although there are spectacular rosettes at Ormaig, there are more in Northumberland, West Yorkshire and High Auchenlarie (Beckensall, 1999, 21). There is nothing like the large cup-less multiple concentric circles at Chapel Stile (Beckensall 2002, 35). There are few arcs, except at Glasvaar. Nowhere are there the ladder motifs of West Yorkshire (Beckensall 1999, 30) or the grid patterns of Galloway, Northumberland and North Yorkshire. Even the rich rock surfaces of Achnabreck do not have every representative motif found in Britain. Nowhere do we find the exotic, 'baroque' style of art of the Irish passage graves and chambered tombs. Neither is it helpful to claim some Kilmartin motifs as being of 'passage grave' type. There are no decorated vertical faces of cliffs like those at Ballochmyle (Beckensall 1999, 67) Hawthornden (NT280 632) or Morwick (Beckensall 1999, 16) that carry a profusion of unusual motifs.

The most significant contexts for rock art are standing stones and burial sites. Like Northumberland, standing stones in this area have cups, with an occasional ring. There is nothing like Cumbrian Long Meg (Beckensall 2002, 59) for lavish ornament. In burial cairns it is only cups that are used, until the metal-type axes are added or the rare linear motifs at Badden and Carn Ban. Motifs in cists vary between those already on outcrop before being removed for cist construction to the purpose-made slabs at Fulforth Farm (page 21) and Pool Farm, West Hamptree (Coles et al, 2000). The latter, recently re-assessed, has a ground-down surface on which there have been pecked twelve cups, six footprints and a possible seventh. The date of the cremations in the cist is from 1890 BC to 1735 BC, the early Bronze Age. Almost all decorated cists in Britain have cups or cup and ring marks, so the presence of footprints, axes, lozenge shapes and lines is rare, so Kilmartin has a fair proportion of the unusual. The introduction of the rare pictorial motifs of axe and footprint appear late in the archaeological record. Temple Wood with its elaborate spiral is a one-off. Galloway, Northumberland, Cumbria and Ireland have a few in burials, on monuments, and in the landscape. West and North Yorkshire, Tayside and Derbyshire have none.

Why does the Kilmartin area have such an appeal? The uncommon motif may manage to capture attention because it is different, but the overall impression is the use to which the most common motifs are put. Their degree of preservation has been ensured by the natural hardness of metamorphic rock. The markings on this would have been a different colour when they were first made, and then blended in with the landscape. Andy McFetters' newly-made motifs at Kilmartin are fresh, but will blend in with the rest of the rock eventually. At 'Brigantium' in Northumberland Clive Waddington's freshly-made motifs have already changed from a pinkish colour to grey.

Distribution

The problem with arranging rock art panels according to their position in the landscape is that no matter how many categories of location are decided, there will be overlaps. However, the distribution of rock art in the Kilmartin region is largely centred on intermediate high places overlooking valleys. It does not appear on the highest ground, and rarely occupies glen floors. The following areas of placement are a guide:

1. There are sites overlooking or close to the sea. To the east are Torradh Na Feinne (although this is probably a portable cist cover), Barr and Brainport Bay. To the west are Poltalloch, Barrackan, Achanarnich, Dun Mhuilig, Ardifuir, Dun Righ and Ormaig.
2. Some rocks are at high places dominating or marking route-ways from and to the sea, including the classic site at Achnabreck.
3. Other route-way sites at high places include Blarbuie; others such as Glasvaar and the Kilmartin sites have a similar position.
4. There are decorated rocks at stream sources, such as Loch Michean (also high in the hills), Allt Bealaich, Ruaidh and Cairnbaan.
5. Most sites overlook glens from slopes, including Dunamuck, Kilmichael Glassary, Glenmoine, Upper Largie, Slockavullin, Ballygowan, Torran, Ford, Finchairn, Eurach, Creagantairbh and some at Kilbride (the others being on the glen floor).
6. Other sites in high places are Dunmore, Kilmory, and Meall a'Bhraithain.
7. Decorated outcrop and a standing stone are on the glen floor at Torbhlaran.
8. Sites related to burials and monuments are at Carn Ban, Badden, Poltalloch North, Nether Largie cairns, Ri Cruin, Baluachraig, Nether Largie standing stones, Temple Wood, and the cist at northern Kilbride.
9. Other sites include two portables at Carnassarie, a 'drowned' boulder at Crinan Ferry and a boulder in a wall at Inverliever. There is a similar boulder in a farm wall at Glasvaar.

An interesting comparison and contrast of the Kilmartin motifs with a new survey of the Loch Tay area helps to throw the distribution of rock art outside monuments and burials into relief. The Royal Commission on the Ancient & Historical Monuments of Scotland surveyed rock art of the Strathtay area in 2000 and identiõed 121 marked rocks where previously there had been only 14. I am grateful to Alex Hale (Hale 2003) for his published account of these decorated rocks, as I was able to record only a small number of them. The loch is long, with steep slopes on either side that are mainly tree-covered. The north slope (south-facing) has a foreshore up to 200m high, and a 1km long terrace between 200-400m high made up of well-drained soils and glacial drift, littered with boulders and with some bedrock outcrops. This terrace is relatively õat to the south and gets steeper to the north. Above 400m the land is bare of trees, with open moorland and three big peat basins. Today it is used for grazing, and in the recent past was used for 'shielings', temporary herds' huts and gardens for summer grazing. The lower and middle slopes are used most today.

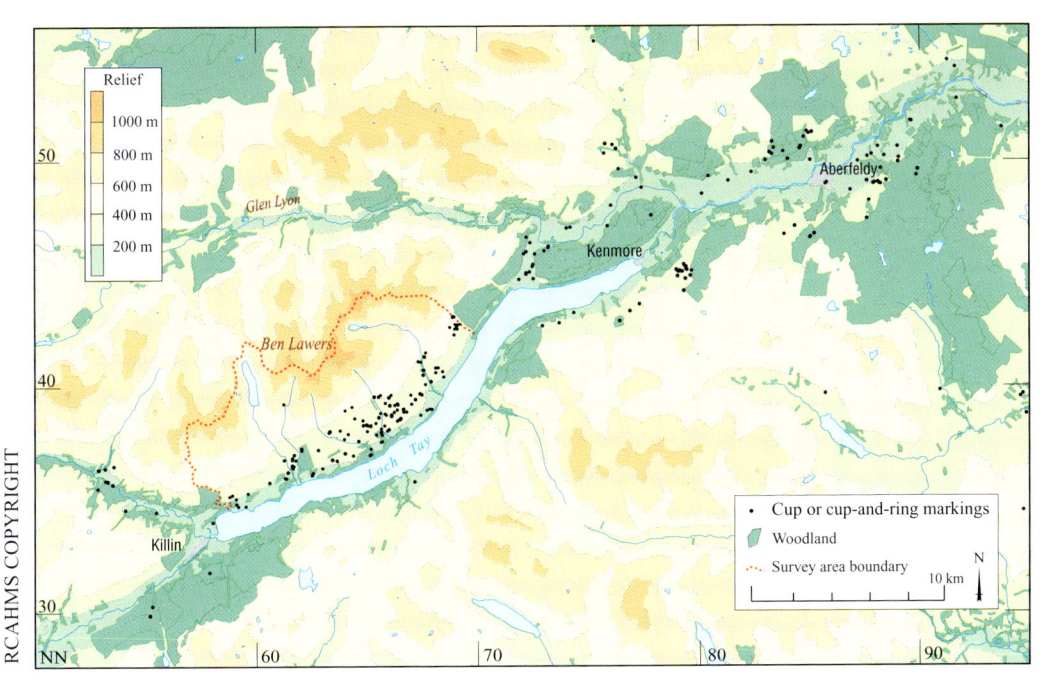

190. Loch Tay Area

The 14 sites previously recorded included 21 cup and ring marked rocks, two of which could not be relocated. The newly discovered sites are in four concentrations, with a dispersed group to the west, a tight group of eight rocks further east, 70 dispersed boulders or decorated bedrock, and 12 rocks at the eastern end. The gaps between the clusters of marked rocks pose some questions: were there any there originally? Have they been removed by farming? Does the dense vegetation of the loch shore cover some? How many have found their way into walls? Alex Hale reported that at least 10% of known marked rocks have been removed: four appear in buildings, three in enclosure banks of dykes (walls), ŏve in clearance heaps and one in a rockery. His analysis shows that of the 121 marked rocks 16 are on bedrock outcrop (3 have cups and rings, the rest plain cups), with four on the lowest and 12 on the middle bands. 105 are on boulders, all in the upper band, with only one cup and single ring rock in the lowest band. All the views from the rocks are naturally to the south and SE, but in the past the views may have been obscured by vegetation (yet to be determined by palynology). On the highest ground there is a concentration of marked rocks at springs and stream sources; lower down, the ground has been cleared for pasture. The marked rocks do not dominate the landscape, and can only be seen from close by. More prominent rocks have no markings on them, so the emphasis is on marking rocks that already blend in with the landscape – assimilation rather than dominance. In dividing types of motifs from one another, Alex Hale has classiŏed them as follows:

1. Single cups: 24 on boulders, one on outcrop
2. Multiple plain cups: on 82 boulders and 13 bedrock sheets (e.g. 5)
3. Multiple cups, some with single rings on 9 boulders and one outcrop
4. Multiple cups, some with multiple rings, on 7 earth-fast rocks and one outcrop. On these 8 rocks 18 cups have more than one ring (eg.1)
5. Multiple cups, some with single or multiple rings and radial ducts. These are on 5 boulders and one outcrop (eg. 2,3,4)

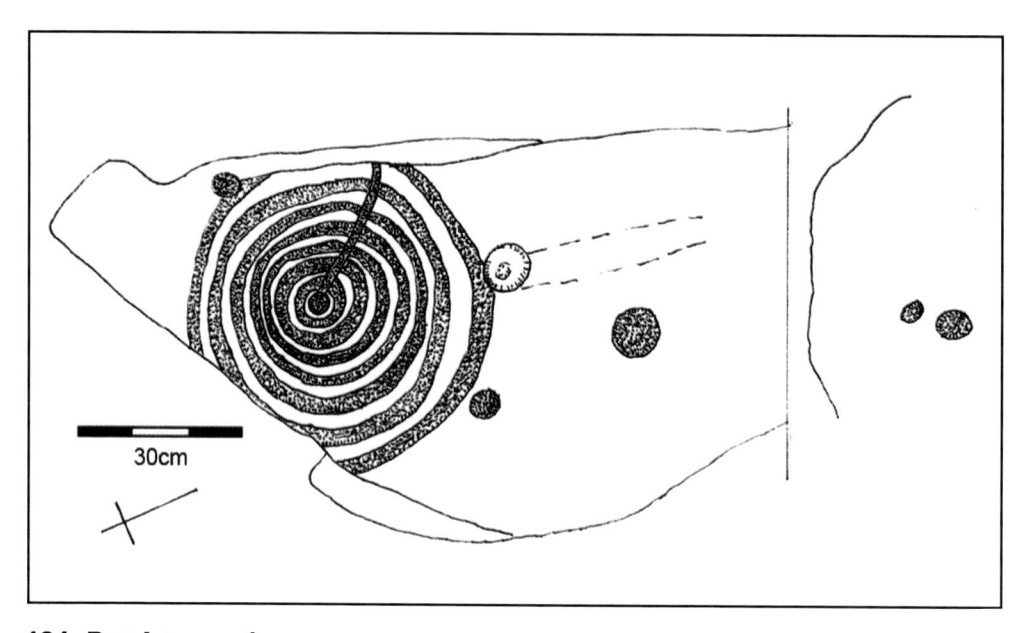

191. Ben Lawers 1

The more elaborate designs show evidence of sequence, additions and alterations that could have been made at any time. Those numbered are illustrated here. The distribution shows most below the head dykes on cultivated land, but the most dramatic designs are on the higher ground. What does this mean? Bearing in mind that ŏnds are often at the whim of individuals, a regulated search like this that has revealed so many new marked rocks makes an assessment more conŏdent. It has been noted, for example, that the marked rocks are related to the boundaries of different soil types, a point that is seldom noted. In the past, as now, vegetation would follow that distribution. In Alex Hales' words: 'they are related to the character of the ground, probably as indicated by the particular type of vegetation.'

Increase in data allows us to reassess previous research, such as that of Margaret Stewart (1959) and Richard Bradley (1993). One conclusion is that the more elaborate rock art in this survey does appear at a higher level than simple cups, but that the latter continue to take their place alongside the former and that the lower ground is not devoid of cups and rings. Another observation is that when we talk about 'complex' motifs, we must remember that one of the panels illustrated here shows how elaborate a pattern can be by using only cups. One particular observation made in Strathtay that linked to our discoveries in County Durham was the coincidence of some marked rocks with stream sources ('viewpoints' in Durham being limited). Another major point is that rock art here blends in with the landscape and tends to avoid the more prominent rocks.

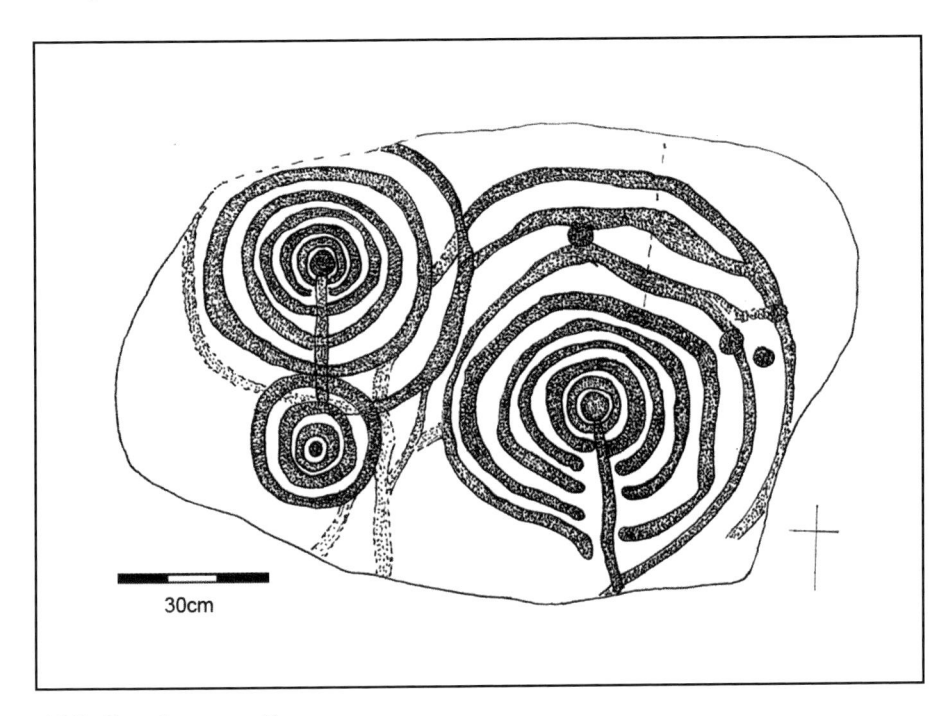

192. Ben Lawers 2

There is intense interest today in the psychology of people who carved rocks in prehistoric times. There is a particularly intriguing question about why on the Continent there are so many picture images whereas in Britain we have non-ŏgurative images. The ŏgurative images, whether in caves or later depictions hammered onto rock surfaces have always attracted more attention, because people think they know where they are with them. They are recognisable. Perhaps with the non-ŏgurative images we need to ignore the physical world if we are to understand them. Some believe that this means reaching into not only the conscious, but into the sub-conscious mind. In areas where there is far more recent rock art stretching back to a distant past and where there is even a recorded memory of those who have created it and used it, such as South Africa (Bushmen) and Australia (Aboriginal), researchers have looked for explanations.

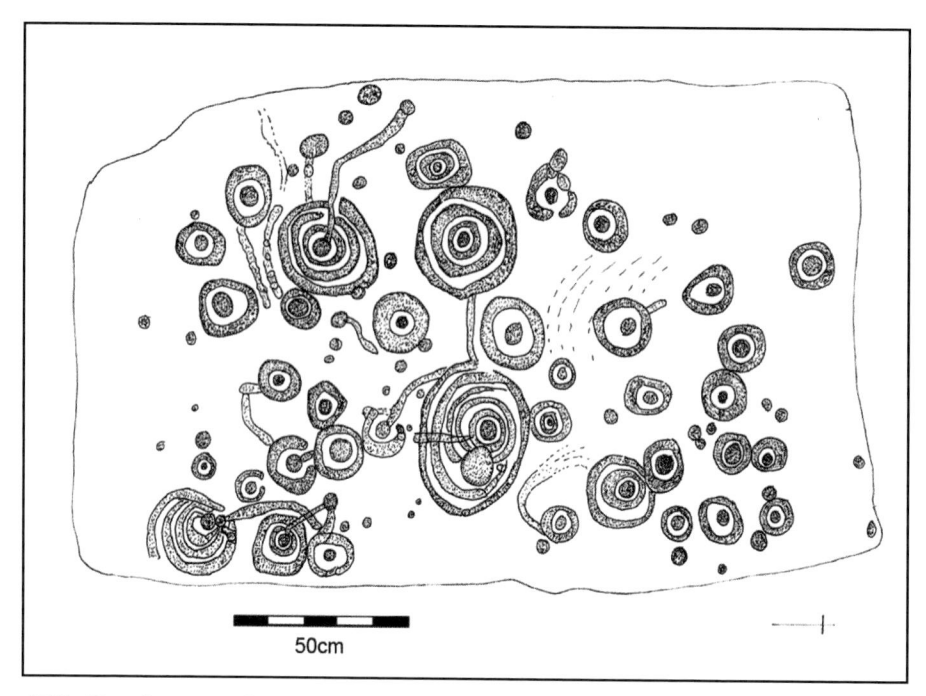

193. Ben Lawers 3

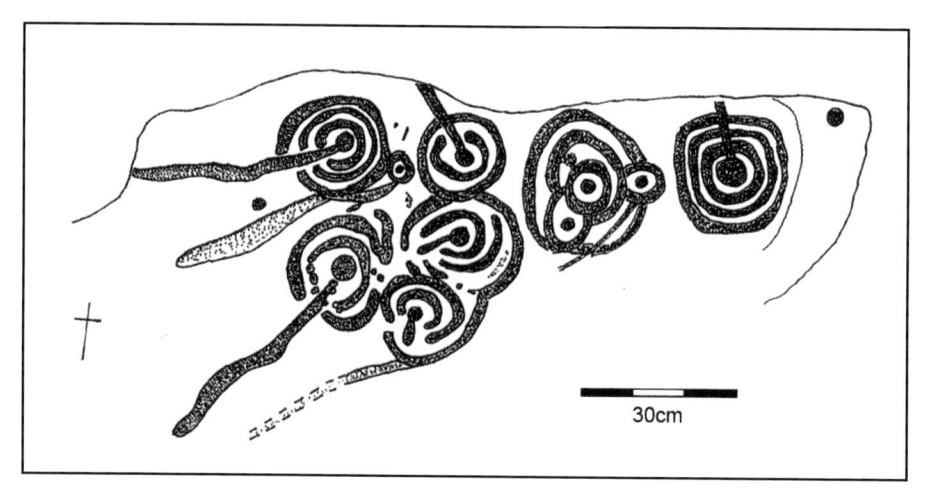

194. Ben Lawers 4

Almost all rock art in monuments, in burials and in the landscape of Britain is non-õgurative. In cup and ring art, there are many variations such as arcs, rectangles, grids and squares that provide variety and can be attributed to an individual seeing it in a different way. The end result is non-representational art. All these variations cannot be demonstrated to have come from nature. We might see ripple marks in pools, zig-zag skylines of hills and trees, the annual rings of a fallen tree, vulvas, breasts or whatever as sources for these images, but where is the evidence that this is what they are? There is, however, a marked difference between the motifs found in passage graves and those in the open air. Whereas the latter sit on outcrop and earth-fast stones, the latter are cut from rock, shaped and ordered in order to ŏt tomb-design. This creates a different impression from art in the landscape, enhanced by the exuberance of the decoration. Art used in later mounds in different areas from these giants has only limited cups and cups and rings incorporated.

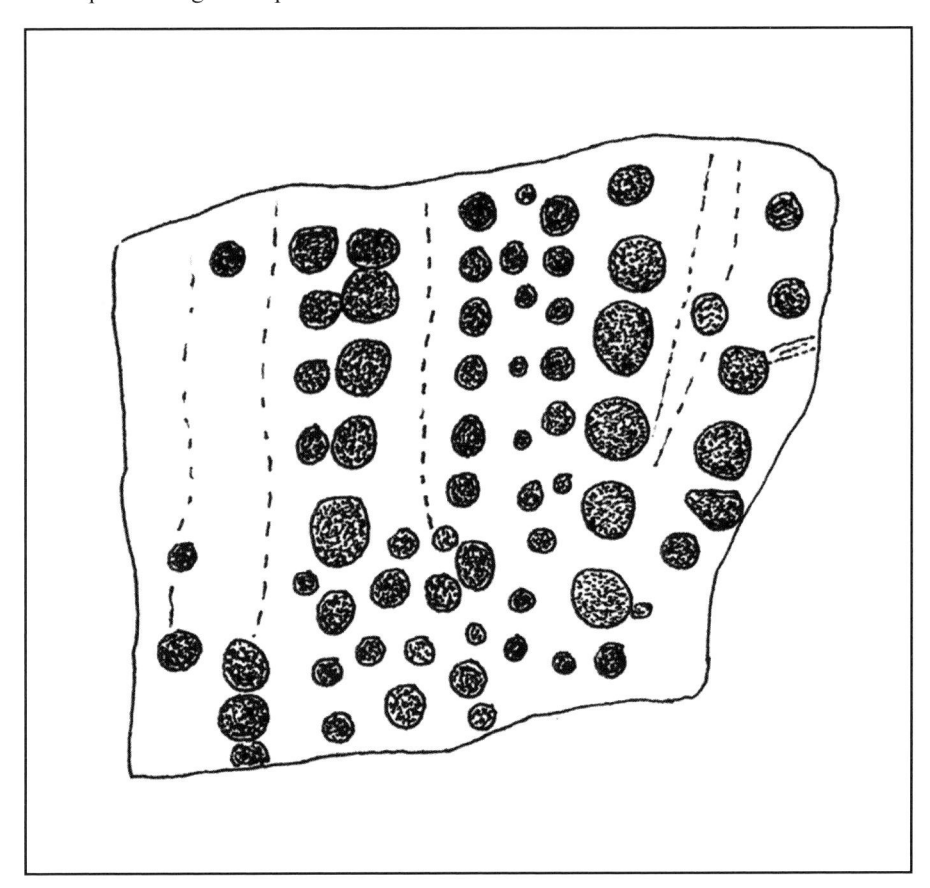

195. Ben Lawers 5

What is the difference, then? Clive Waddington (Waddington 2004) in a recent investigation has made a convincing case for two separate traditions. Passage grave art occurs close to the sea and river estuaries in Atlantic Europe, such as Anglesey and Portugal. In Ireland 84% are in County Meath with access to the sea, mostly close to the River Boyne, and, like those in the Orkneys, have been dated to the late 4th and early 3rd Millennium BC. Does this mean that groups of people who perhaps originated in the same lands and who thought alike were responsible? Cup and ring marks occur in different areas from these; there is no passage grave art in Kilmartin or Tayside, but plenty of the other. These tombs have a different function in cave-like ritual from landscape art, which is much more widespread and, presumably, accessible.

196. Passage grave art at Newgrange, Ireland.

There is a clear difference in the form of the motifs. Patterns of lozenge-shapes, spirals, zigzags and wavy lines are also present on pottery. There is an early pottery style called Grooved Ware spread all over Britain that shares some of these motifs, and this is associated with open-air 'ritual' sites around passage graves and henges. Style, however, is only one strand in the reasons for the difference between passage grave and open-air art. If we choose to go by design alone, we may ŏnd linear designs and lozenge

197. Irish passage grave art at Loughcrew.

shapes on Food Vessels, Beakers and Urns, but as these vessels are from c.2000 BC and passage graves are hundreds of years earlier, this demonstrates the dangers of making comparisons. Also this pottery exists widely where there is no rock art. Given that the passage grave tradition is so different in use and space, Clive Waddington concludes that the shared similarities between passage tomb regions, the artwork, the chronologies, and their distribution along the Atlantic seaboard of Europe suggests that the idea of passage grave art in Ireland and western Britain is, perhaps, in origin, intrusive.

Coping with theories: a warning

The absurdity of playing a game of origins and meanings makes some popular television. Think of the Crop Circle circus, and the contention that Stonehenge's Heel Stone was the penis of the Sky God and when it cast its shadow inside the horseshoe at Stonehenge it was fertilising the Earth Mother. In an attempt to authenticate this, viewers were shown a sacred cave which resembled female reproductive organs. So what? It is nonsense like this, and the apparent endorsement by respectable archaeologists that obscures reality. We all have our gut-reaction theories, but most of us grow out of them in the cold light of truth.

The term 'abstract art' comes from inside the mind, but 'representational art' comes from natural forms that we see around us. I have in the past loosely called rock art images 'abstract', but feel inclined to reconsider the terminology. Non-representational images seems better. My own ideas on the origins of basic forms such as spirals and concentric circles have by no means been universally popular. I have noted that children have a strong tendency to draw them as though they are deeply embedded in their minds (consciousness). It seems like a natural process, the same way that they draw adults around them at an early age as creatures with small heads and enormous legs and arms – an understandable view of a world in which they are so small.

Some archaeologists believe that rock art images are produced in a state of altered consciousness, in a heightened state of excitement and awareness. It goes like this: people had trance visions and acquired the images that they depicted – circles, zig-zags, wavy lines, for example – that occur in rock art all over the world because these images are in their consciousness waiting to be released. Such images are common to all humans and are rooted in the brain or nervous system (entoptic). Some of these are seen by migraine sufferers (during my own rare attacks of migraine wavy lines appear at the edges of my vision).

So how do these images come to the surface? One way in which our minds are relaxed and made receptive is through trance. This can be brought about by the action of the group on an individual or individuals through dance or by other rhythmic stimuli such as clapping. Party-goers who don't drink alcohol can get high on the mood created by a party and their behaviour becomes more relaxed. Mobs can stir up normally placid people to act in a way that they would not normally endorse. This does not have to be spelt out further, but action, as hypnotists are aware, cannot be aroused in someone who is deeply opposed to it. Society has people to whom the group can turn when it is difocult to cope. People who cannot face the death of a loved one may turn to spiritualists to re-connect them. A family doctor or priest become a lifeline. People turn to horoscopes or go through rituals like throwing salt over the shoulder to ward off bad luck. All this happens in so-called civilised society, where fear and superstition still lurk below the surface. In primitive societies a person with unusual perceptions, sometimes known as a 'shaman', is identiőed as the helper in times of acute stress. These people are not charlatans; much illness is mental, affecting bodily function, and helping the mind to cope and hope and think positively is a vital service. In some societies the shaman may go into a state of trance in order to enter a spirit world where help is available and return with an answer. This trance state may be induced by group inouence, or it may be assisted or induced by taking drugs. Drugs alter the state of consciousness, and some believe that during this state of surrender people see the kinds of images that occur in rock art. No doubt my oversimpliőcation of the process may not do justice to it. Some who strongly believe this have used drugs themselves to test the hypothesis, but as I am unwilling to experiment beyond moderate alcohol consumption, my perceptions are limited.

I can believe that locked up inside our brain or nerve centres are basic images common to all people, and that what we see on the rocks may have stemmed from some release. How else can we account for the universal use of symbols such as cups, concentric rings, spirals, zig-zags and lozenge shapes? To see that a panel of rock art in California could be equally at home in Kilmartin points to some common inspiration oceans and continents apart. People do not have to meet in Britain to decide to put spirals on cliffs in Northumberland or in Temple Wood, or to put rosettes on rocks overlooking the sea at Ormaig or on outcrops in Northumberland.

The distribution of rock art over Britain is hardly surprising when seen against the similarity in styles of pottery, artefacts, house construction, and farming methods. Neither is it surprising that rock art in Galicia is so much like that in Britain, for the sea has never been an insuperable barrier. What is difőcult to account for is the virtual absence of rock art in the south of England from where so many other ideas could have spread. It may have taken a more perishable form, and may have been inhibited by a lack of suitable rock surfaces, but it is still odd. Against that we must take into account that it was by no means widespread in northern Britain. It is scattered thinly in parts, and there are more concentrated patches in others. It does occur in burials, but why should Ireland house the greatest passage grave tombs with their art? For those who believe in those tombs as being created by intoxicated shamans I direct them to George Eogan, the man who has excavated them for years and who knows them all intimately. When he was interviewed for *Current Archaeology* (CA October 2203) by Andrew Selkirk with the question "Do you believe in these current ideas about it being inspired by shamans under the inouence of drugs?" he paused slightly, said "No", then changed the subject.

The issue remains open, and is likely to do so no matter how far the theory applies to other cultures at others times. There is no direct evidence of the presence of shamans or of their inouence on rock art in Britain. We may look for such evidence, but what can we possibly expect to őnd?

13. The future of Rock Art studies

Never before has rock art received such attention from so many people in so many parts of the world. The range of people interested is extraordinary - from those with a casual interest to academics who have chosen to study it in depth. Kilmartin has already faced many implications of having an important rock art resource in its landscape and monuments. Work on it has included excavation and recording, display and publication. Across the Border, the English Heritage Rock Art Pilot Project was designed to investigate these issues. Scottish, Welsh and Irish rock art specialists were invited onto the Advisory Committee, for the research and its implications should apply to the whole of Britain.

Recording

Naturally, one priority of the survey was to find out exactly how much was known already. There are many sources, including books and papers, and many regions have a Sites and Monuments Record of what is on their patch. However, it soon became clear that the standard of recording was variable, and there was a need to produce an agreed common standard. Here follows a summary of some of the issues raised:

The places where rock art is found can be accurately plotted with the aid of GPS. This is far removed from the days when people entered the field with chains and compasses in a time-consuming process to plot sites on a map.

Rock art has to be drawn and photographed. That sounds straight-forward, but isn't. A glance at many reports will show that some drawings are free-hand and approximate. There is little attempt to show the natural structure of a rock surface, with its cracks and indentations; drawings in thick or thin black lines take no account of the relationships between one motif and another. For example, some motifs are fainter than others, and there are some traces of superimposition of symbols and motifs. No attempt even today has been made to find a way of recording the varied depths of cups and grooves. Professor John Coles, who has done extensive work developing recording systems in Scandinavia, writes: 'I suggest that the days of simple black and white illustration, devoid of structure and variation, should now be drawn to a conclusion'. He also suggests that any system should include 'the depth of the carvings'. (Coles 2003).

Modern technology can help here, for the laser scanner shows each motif clearly and presents a contour picture of the rock, including the varying depth of the grooves. This can certainly be done now with panels that are accessible, and more remote sites may follow later. As laser scanning is expensive and not applied universally, other methods of recording are still used and can be very accurate.

Wax-rubbing in which black wax is rubbed on the surface of thin, strong newsprint, is a method that I have used to great effect, but this is an acquired skill; without plenty of practice and patience this can be subjective. Many systems of recording suffer from the operator making assumptions about the way the pattern is developing, and may be wrong. Even with the most careful rubbing on paper over a clean surface, the results must be checked against photographs taken in strong, oblique light, preferably not at one time or season only.

If the rubbings, which are a primary source of information, are to be stored, there may be a problem with the type of paper used. Many advocate acid-free paper, but this is expensive. The whole purpose is not to produce decorative wall-coverings but to provide a basis for an accurate drawing. In most cases this is perfectly possible, but as the surface of a rock undulates and dips, there is bound to be a distortion of area when it is reduced to a ơat surface.

The rubbing may be covered with a grid of 10cm squares so that the information can be transferred to graph paper, giving a scale of 1/10. Then the drawing is made, with further reference to photographs and to further visits to the site to check all details. Symbols have to be devised so that natural markings are distinguished from artiőcial. Wherever motifs are clearly spaced there is no problem; where and how motifs merge must be shown. This method of recording is not infallible, and may only be applied to Scheduled Ancient Monuments with express permission.

Another method is to cover the rock with a sheet of polythene and use a felt pen to draw the design. This sounds satisfactory, but is less objective than a rubbing. Motifs cannot be easily seen under plastic unless they have been őlled in with some substance beforehand; this reads the pattern decided by the eye onto the tracing. Corrections can be made, however, to the őnal drawing in the light of good photographs and through selective rubbings of difőcult areas. A glance at any report from anywhere in the world shows that there are many methods of drawing. Some use dark grooves against a white background; others have white grooves against a stippled or shaded background. Some put in a sharp edge to cups and rings; others a fuzzy edge. There is as yet no agreed single method. The key question is what detailed information is a drawing expected to give?

Even when drawings are good, they still need to be complemented by good photographs. Black and white is an excellent medium, and those taken years ago outlive colour prints. Today's technology allows colour prints to be turned into black and white, and colour itself can be enhanced and adjusted. Digital images are particularly useful in close-ups and do not require a great deal of light, although oblique sunlight shows details better. There is a standard scale now accepted, produced by IFRAO, that shows not only centimetres but colours. In the past we have all been in the őeld when, for various reasons, an acceptable scale has not been available, and coins, walking sticks, pencils, spectacles, buckets, combs and anything handy have been used as scale. In time these will come to date the photographs! Information that accompanies the drawings and photography must include details of the area and its recorded archaeology. The type of rock must be noted too, and the presence of growths on the rock such as lichen – establishing the rock's 'history'.

A 360-degree photographic image around a rock is desirable, and there are special lenses for this.

The most thorough and effective system of recording in the UK has been developed at Newcastle University. This is not the place to examine it in detail, but it meets all the criteria of the precision that is required (Mazel 2003, ongoing). It is able to accommodate all regions of Britain and abroad in a coherent, universal system, although its scope is at the time of writing conõned to Northumberland. As the Newcastle Museum of Antiquities has a large hidden cache of prehistoric marked rocks, one aim is to extend museum and other facilities to encourage everyone to use the information. That said, an English Heritage Report (2000) states that. "It would be better to achieve complete coverage at a standard level (that later could be enhanced if resources became available) rather than attain partial cover at a de luxe level in some areas and nothing at all in others". That would be all very well, but as little has happened to achieve this since the report was written, it is better to support the real work being done and build on that.

197. A new discovery by Barbara Brown in North Yorkshire.

Threats to rock art

The dangers to rock art must be assessed. In Britain human intervention, particularly in the form of quarrying and farming has led to the destruction of many panels or to their defacement. A priority is to ensure that those we know about should be legally and scientifically protected. Another threat to decorated rocks is a natural one: that exposure opens up some rocks to the action of water, frost, acid rain and the growth of lichens. In the latter case we are still not sure what effect lichens have. It seems logical that, if they grow on a rock surface, they are drawing out minerals to feed on. On the other hand, the cover that lichens and mosses provided may protect the rock from other kinds of erosion. There is a clear need for an objective study.

As rock art has become so popular throughout the world to visitors, this popularity is both a blessing and a danger. That people wish to share a heritage is laudable, but some still wish to add their names and scrawls as a cheap sort of immortality. We see names, initials and dates chiselled into the rocks at such places as Ormaig. That this is not general in the Kilmartin area is partly due to making people aware of the importance and fragility of the motifs, and by satisfying their needs by providing controlled access. This is a management problem shared by all historical sites. In Scotland there is considerable work being done to assess and remedy any threats to decorated surfaces, not only on prehistoric sites but at all places where stonework, marked or not, is in danger. An important document on this, Carved Stones: Historic Scotland's Approach, set out the store in 2003.

Conservation and Management

Conservation and management go hand in hand. Monument status theoretically gives a rock legal protection, but that does not protect it. I know of many rocks that have been removed, and have reported this. Protection involves making intelligent decisions on which panels are best displayed and which should be covered over. Is the action of weather eroding the marks? That sounds an easy question to answer, but it isn't, for the time of the year or day when markings are viewed makes them appear strong or faint. There has to be a more objective method.

How often are marked rocks visited by inspectors? Infrequently at present; never in some places. This is where a local involvement is important: people who care enough to visit ought to report anything worrying. It is more desirable to have regional groups made responsible rather than distant bureaucracy, and for these groups to form a larger network for the purposes of standardisation. Rock art must get its fair share of the budget for such work; we pay for its protection out of our taxes. It is easy to overlook such a small part of our heritage when spending millions on upstanding architecture. Such an important part of our history, and such an intriguing mystery draws thousands to visit Kilmartin and similar sites every year, but too much may be left to chance. We need to publicise it more, to make it more generally available, especially to children and schools. When people are directed to sites, the sites must be displayed to the highest standards of interpretation and good taste.

In the field it is important that rock art should not be seen as something detached from the landscape as a whole. The Kilmartin House Museum has played a vital part in encouraging people to take an intelligent interest in the area by interpreting what can be seen there. In this way people realise how important it is to cherish and preserve rock art, an essential and intriguing part of our history. In this, Kilmartin is an ideal situation, as one views it alongside other prehistoric remains. A tour of the well-displayed panels takes in so much of the landscape around it and gives the visitor a strong sense of place. The trail can be extended. At the same time other demands on the landscape are evident: forestry, quarrying, arable and livestock farming. It is essential to get a balance between the needs of tourism and industry. It is hard for a farmer whose sheep are lambing to have to face a problem of uncontrolled visitors' dogs crossing the field. The lessons that we have learnt in Britain and continue to learn through selective excavation and site management may be shared with the rest of the world, and we can learn much from the experience of other countries. We must be uncompromising in reaching for the highest standards. The past deserves it and the future expects it of us.

What is left for us to see is what we can delight in. The places where rock art occurs, often remote, needing effort to find, can be extraordinary in their beauty. There is a strong sense of place, of the past, of a mystery. The markings themselves, such an integral part of the landscape, can be profuse and varied or of incredible simplicity, where a single cup mark must have had powerful meaning. It is as important to our heritage as monuments that may well dwarf it and shout for our attention. Rock art intrigues not only by its presence but also by its provocation. 'You don't and you can't know everything, for all your searching', it seems to say, but it gently prods us to go on with the quest for knowledge.

14. Bibliography

Books and papers listed below will contain guides to additional sources of information.
General surveys
Bahn, P. (Ed)   1991. Rock Art and Prehistory. (Oxford, Oxbow).
Bahn, P. 1998. The Cambridge Illustrated History of Prehistoric Art (Cambridge UP).
Beckensall, S. with T. Laurie. 1998. Prehistoric Rock Art of County Durham, Swaledale and Wensleydale. (County Durham Books, Durham County Council)
Beckensall, S. 1999 British Prehistoric Rock Art. (Tempus). Hardback
Beckensall, S. 2001 Northumberland: the Power of Place (Tempus)
Beckensall, S. 2001 Prehistoric Rock Art in Northumberland. (Tempus)
Beckensall, S. 2002 Prehistoric Rock Art in Cumbria. (Tempus).
Beckensall, S. 2002 British Prehistoric Rock Art (Tempus). Paperback.
Beckensall, S. 2003 Prehistoric Northumberland (Tempus)
Boughey, K.J.S. and Vickerman, E.A. 2003. Prehistoric Rock Art of the West Riding. (Yorkshire Archaeology 9, West Yorkshire Archaeology Service)
Bradley, R. 1993. Altering the Earth. (Edinburgh).
Bradley, R. 1997. Rock Art and the Prehistory of Atlantic Europe. (Routledge).
Bradley, R. 1998. The Significance of Monuments. (Routledge).
Brown, P. and Chappell, G. Forthcoming. Prehistoric Rock Art of North Yorkshire. (Tempus)
Burl, A. 1999. The Stone Circles of the British Isles. (Yale).
English Heritage   2000. Rock Art Pilot Project Report. (Limited circulation)
Chippindale, C. and Tacon, S.C. (Eds.) 1998. The Archaeology of Rock-Art. (Cambridge)
Eogan, G. 1986. Knowth and the Passage Tombs of Ireland. (London: Thames and Hudson)
Eogan, G. 1984 and 1997. Excavations at Knowth Vols. 1 and 2. (Royal Irish Academy)
Hadingham, E. 1974. Ancient Carvings in Britain: A Mystery. (London).
Ilkley Archaeological Group 1986. The Carved Rocks on Rombalds Moor. (Wakefield).
Lewis-Williams, D. 2002. The Mind in the Cave. (Thames and Hudson)
Morris, RWB. 1977. The Prehistoric Rock Art of Argyll. (Poole).
Morris, RWB. 1981. The Prehistoric Rock Art of Galloway and the Isle of Man. (Poole).
Morris, RWB. 1981. The Prehistoric Rock Art of Southern Scotland. BAR. Series 86. (Oxford)
Nash, G. and Chippindale, C. (Eds.) 2002. European Landscapes of Rock-Art. (Routledge)
O'Kelly, M. 1982. Newgrange. Archaeology, Art and Legend. (London. Thames and Hudson)
RCHMS 1988. Argyll, Vol. 6. (Edinburgh: HMSO)
Shee Twohig, E. 1981. The Megalithic Art of Western Europe. (Oxford).

Shee Twohig, E. and Ronane, M. (Eds). Past Perceptions: The prehistoric archaeology of south-west Ireland. (University of Cork Press)
Simpson, J. 1867. Archaic Sculpturings of Cups, Circles etc upon Stones and rocks in Scotland, England etc and other Countries. (Edinburgh, Edmonston and Douglas).
Van Hoek, MAM. 1995. Morris' Prehistoric Rock Art of Galloway. (Oisterwijk, Privately printed)

General articles:

References to Prehistoric Rock Art are often scattered, but there are some journals that have recorded new finds and published valuable contributions to Prehistory generally. These include:

The Antiquaries Journal. London
Archaeologia Aeliana. Newcastle upon Tyne.
British Archaeology. Council for British Archaeology.
Cambridge Archaeological Journal
Current Archaeology. London.
Discovery and Excavation in Scotland (DES) (Council for British Arcaheology)
Durham Archaeological Journal
Glasgow Archaeological Journal
Northern Archaeology. Northumberland Archaeological Group. Newcastle upon Tyne.
Oxford Journal of Archaeology
Proceedings of the Society of Antiquaries of Scotland. Edinburgh.
Proceedings of the Prehistoric Society.
Transactions of the Cumberland and Westmorland Antiquarian and Archaeological Society.
Yorkshire Archaeological Journal

Some general and specific articles on Prehistoric rock art include:

Allen, R. 1881. Notes on some un-described stones with cup-markings in Scotland. (PSAS XVI).
Barnatt, J. and Reeder, P. 1982. Prehistoric rock art in the Peak District.
(Derbyshire Arch. Journal 102,33-44)
Barnatt, J. and Robinson, F. 2003. Prehistoric Rock Art in Ashover School and Further New Discoveries elsewhere in the Peak District. (Derbyshire AJ.Vol. 123).
Beckensall, S. 1995. Recent Discovery and Recording of Prehistoric Rock Motifs in the North. (Northern Archaeology. 12. Newcastle)
Beckensall, S. and Frodsham, P. 1998. Questions of Chronology: the case for Bronze Age Rock Art in Northern England. (Northern Archaeology. 15/16. Newcastle)
Beckensall, S. 1997. Symbols on Stone: the State of the Art. (Council for Independent Archaeology).
Beckensall, S. 1997. Prehistoric Rock Art-Progress and Problems. (At the Edge. No. 8).
Beckensall, S. 1999. Art on the Rocks. (3rd Stone. No 35).
Bradley, R. 1996. Learning from Places – Topographical Analysis of Northern British Rock Art. (Northern Archaeology. 13/14. Newcastle).
Bradley, R., Harding, J., and Matthews, M. 1993. The Siting of Prehistoric rock art in Galloway, South-West Scotland. (PPS. 59)
Burgess, C. 1990. The chronology of cup and ring marks in Britain and Ireland. (Northern Archaeology. Newcastle).
Campbell, M. and Sandeman, M. 1964. Mid Argyll: an Archaeological Survey. (PSAS XCV 1-125).
Campbell, M, Scott J.G, and Piggott S. 1960. The Badden Slab. (PSAS XCIV).

Campbell, M. 1965. In Discovery and Excavation in Scotland.

Christison, D. 1903. On the standing stones and cup-marked rocks etc. in the Valley of the Add. (PSAS XXXVIII)

Coles, J, Gestdottir, H, and Minnitt, S. 2000. A Bronze Age decorated Cist Cover from Pool Farm, West Harptree: New Analyses. (Somerset Archaeology and Natural History Society).

Coles, J., 2003. A measure of conviction: recording emphasis in Scandinavian rock carvings. (Antiquity 77 297)

Craw, J.H. 1929. A Jet necklace from a cist at Poltalloch. (PSAS. LXIII).

Craw, J.H. 1931. Further Excavations of cairns at Poltalloch. (PSAS LXV).

Frodsham, P. 1996. Spirals in Time: Morwick Mill and the Spiral Motif in the British Neolithic. (Northern Archaeology. 13/14. Newcastle).

Hale, A. 2003. Prehistoric rock carvings in Strath Tay. (Tayside and Fife Archaeological Journal. Volume 9)

Heaney, S. 1990. New Selected Poems 1966-1987. (Faber)

Hewitt, I. 1991. Prehistoric rock motifs in Great Britain. (Unpublished research thesis, Bournemouth University).

Historic Scotland Archaeology Paper. 2003. Carved Stones: Historic Scotland's Approach. (Historic Scotland)

Johnston, S. 1993. The relationship between prehistoric Irish rock art and Irish passage tomb art. (OJA, 12)

Mackie, E. and Davis, A. 1989. New light on Neolithic rock carvings: the petroglyphs at Greenland (Auchentorlie) Dumbartonshire. (Glasgow Archaeological Journal, 15).

Morris, RWB. 1989. The Prehistoric Rock Art of Great Britain: a survey of all sites bearing motifs more complex than simple cup marks. (PPS.Vol.55).

Morris, RWB and Bailey, D.C. 1964. Cup-and-ring marks of SW Scotland. (PSAS. XCVIII).

Morris, RWB 1967. Cup-and ring marks…part 2 (PSAS 100).

Morris, RWB 1970. The Petroglyphs of Achnabreck. (PSAS 103).

O'Sullivan, M. 1989. A stylistic revolution in the megalithic art of the Boyne valley (Archaeology Ireland. 3.4)

O'Kelley, C. 1973. Passage grave art in the Boyne valley. PPS. 39. 354-382.

Powell, T. and Daniel, G. 1956. Barclodiad y Gawres. (Liverpool UP).

Ritchie, J.N.G, 1974. Excavation of the stone circle and cairn at Balbirnie, Fife. (AJ 131, 1-32).

Scott, J. 1989. The stone circles at Temple Wood, Kilmartin, Argyll. (GAJ.15)

Selkirk, A. 2003. Eogan of Knowth. (Current Archaeology. 188)

Sharples, N. 1984. Excavations at Pierowall quarry, Westray, Orkney. (PSAS. 114, 75-125).

Sherriff, J.1995.Prehistoric rock-carvings in Angus. (Tayside and Fife Archaeological Journal 1,11-22).

Simpson, D. and Thawley, J. 1972. Single Grave Art in Britain. (Scottish Archaeological Forum, 4).

Spratt, D.A. 1982. Prehistoric and Roman Archaeology of North-East Yorkshire (BAR 104)

Stevenson, J. 1993. Cup and ring markings at Ballochmyle, Ayrshire, (GAJ. 11).

Stevenson, J.1997, The Prehistoric Rock Carvings of Argyll, in G. Richie (ed.) The Archaeology of Argyll. Edinburgh. 95-117.

Stewart M. 1958. Strath Tay in the second millennium BC- a field survey. (PSAS 92, 71-84).

Waddington, C. 1996. Putting Rock Art to Use. A model of Early Neolithic Transhumance in North Northumberland. (Northern Archaeology. 13/14. Newcastle).

Waddington, C. 1998. Cup and Ring Marks in Context. (CAJ 8,No.1, 29-54).

Waddington, C. 2004. Forthcoming article on Cups and Rings and passage Grave Art.

In time for the publication of this book are three European international publications which include articles by the author:
Stan Beckensall. *British Rock Art* in 2004. The Valcamonica Symposiums 2001 and 2002 (National Heritage Board of Sweden)
Stan Beckensall. *British Prehistoric Rock Art* in 2004, The Future of Rock Art – a World Review (National Heritage Board of Sweden)
Stan Beckensall. The Significance of the distribution of rock art in Britain in 2004, XXI Valcamonica Symposium: New discoveries, new interpretations, new research methods. (Centro Camuno di Studi Preistorici)
Readers' attention is also drawn to up to date publications of research in Adoranten (Scandinavian Society for Prehistoric Art), including articles by the author.

There is also an important new website: The Beckensall Northumberland Archive, launched by Newcastle University in January 2005.
http://rockart.ncl.ac.uk

The Kilmartin House Museum has its own website
http://www.kht.org.uk

Acknowledgements
1. I have been lucky to have had the RCAHMS published survey of most of the sites that appear in this book available to check my information and drawings. I am particularly grateful to Jack Stevenson and Alex Hale.
2. I am grateful to Professors Richard Bradley and John Coles, Dr. Aron Mazel and Dr. Clive Waddington for their comments on chapters 12 and 13.
3. The final production of this book would have the poorer without the editorial skills of Georgina Hobhouse, and we owe a great debt to her. The excellent maps are the work of Roddy Regan, whom I also thank. The team at Kilmartin House, led by Sharon Webb, is a talented and formidable one.
4. Finally, I am particularly grateful to Paul and Barbara Brown for their considerable input in the research for this book.